BEYOND FELLOWSHIP: A PRACTICAL GUIDE TO USING THE 12 STEPS FOR ANY RECOVERY

BEYOND FELLOWSHIP: A PRACTICAL GUIDE TO USING THE 12 Steps FOR ANY RECOVERY

PAUL MOORE

ULTIMATE
Vida

"Above all, don't lie to yourself. The man who lies to himself and listens to his own lie comes to a point that he cannot distinguish the truth within him, or around him, and so loses all respect for himself and for others. And having no respect he ceases to love."

- Fyodor Dostoevsky, The Brothers Karamazov

CONTENTS

ACKNOWLEDGMENTS

First and foremost, I'd like to acknowledge that this book couldn't have been possible without my lifelong partner in marriage and life. Her name, directly translated from Portuguese, is grace of Jesus, and it couldn't have been more fitting. She never gave up on me and saw within me things I couldn't see in myself. I'd also thank my wonderful children and grandchildren for forgiving me and sharing in my life.

Next, I'd like to acknowledge those who mentored me from sick to healthy. Jason Hemstreet, Michael Cartwright, and so many others shared their strength and wisdom with patience, love, humility, tolerance, and compassion. The fellowship and steps of Alcoholics Anonymous, without which I may be dead or languishing in prison.

My kind editor Melissa Drake christened me into the process of editing and publishing. Her patience knows no bounds.

Last but certainly not least is my thanks to a loving Higher Power who has made my recovery possible.

Introduction

I'll start simply by saying this is not a replacement for the fellowship and program of the 12 Steps. Instead, it is an augmentation of the capabilities and scope of ways the 12 Steps can be used. The 12 Steps, and the mentors I've had within that fellowship, have saved my life time and time again. I have seen some examples of the erroneous practice of this program, which I have personally experienced, limiting the effectiveness of its use. I'd save anyone who needs this to change their life some of the bad experiences I've had over the years of trying to perfect my process. I believe the goal of overall wellness should be equanimity of mind, peace of mind, and an overall thriving life filled with joy and happiness.

I'm taking a page out of one of my favorite writer's books as I compile my thoughts. Wayne Dyer has long been an inspiration to me in the journey of self-discovery. When he wrote his immensely popular book, *Your Erroneous Zones*, he quit his job and wrote the whole book during a stay in a hotel. While I'm not in a hotel, nor have I quit my day job, I've settled in for a long-needed self-care weekend in an Airbnb. I must have manifested this place somehow. Its eclectic style has a charming air of home. Nothing matches, and yet everything fits together perfectly. The reading materials provided by the homeowner could almost be a handpicked library of my making. The decor is American Pickers meets New England. I feel delighted here in this place at this moment. I'm attired in sweatpants, a North Face® orange hat, and my Hogwarts hoodie. The air on my skin is a temperate 68 degrees Fahrenheit. My focus is present-minded, and my worries are nonexistent. You'll discover this feeling of comfort in my own skin was very hard to win, and therefore I'll do whatever I need to do to keep it. I hit the grocery store for comfort provisions: mini strawberry swirl cheesecake, Tostitos, Doritos, hot bean dip, queso, salsa, sour cream, Mexican blend cheese for nachos, large cooked shrimp cocktail, hot cocktail sauce, three types of Ben and Jerry's Ice cream, Dunkin Donuts coffee, half and half, and last but certainly not least, Toffee Fiddle Faddle. I've prepared for my comfort.

Self-care is neither selfish nor uncaring. It is simply loving myself enough to take care of myself, so I can be there for those who need me. I'll talk more about self-care in upcoming chapters. Plus, mindfulness and those subjects that took me from homelessness, addiction, mental illness, suicidal ideations, and my earnest attempts to achieve the state I presently enjoy. I've lived within a thirty-minute ride of the beach my whole life. I considered titling this book, *Learning to Surf.* That being said, I'm not a surfer. I've never learned to surf—as of yet. I use this metaphor based on the enjoyment and lifestyle in tune with nature and laid back I've heard so many surfers talk about. Do they wipe out occasionally? Of course, they do. But, they pick up, move on, and don't let it ruin their day. The same is true for me and the waves of my journey. Life didn't stop the ocean's waves. It never does. The 12 step program of AA helped me not to drown in addiction. I needed to continue the work because energy cannot be destroyed, and time marches forward.

I simply had to learn to enjoy the waves. I had to learn to surf life. I did that by working on the 12 Steps, and going beyond them while connecting with others.

Life and the enjoyment of it is possible. It's *Beyond Fellowship.*

A journal best accompanies this book. There are spaces for writing within the book, but a practice of journaling is ideal for the best results. Regular journaling will get you in the process of gaining insights into your thinking process. You needn't spend hours a day journaling. A good process and habit can begin in just five or ten minutes a day.

"All the peace, joy, love, and creativity that people could want are closer than we ever imagine. They are our very nature, merely veiled by what we think we know."

— *Andrew Seaton*

CHAPTER ONE

The Most Important Question

Who am I and Why am I Writing This Book?

My name is Paul Moore, and names are important. My last name came from the man who legitimized my mother's pregnancy. I found this out at about 14 years of age. Somehow, I knew what my mother planned to tell me ahead of her actually telling me. Mr. Moore was never a part of my life, nor was my biological father. After long years apart, I have since met and developed a relationship with a half-sister. I grew up first with my mother and was primarily raised by my grandmother shortly after that. We were lower-middle class and the struggle to survive was real. We didn't always have what I wanted to eat in the house. I like cookies, french fries, ketchup, and other savory and sweet delights. Food was my first source of comfort. Later, I disappeared into reading as a comforting get away from reality. My aunt read to me often and fostered a love of this escape.

What was I escaping, you might ask? Not having all the delectable morsels a chubby child could wish for doesn't sound half bad. I was a very sensitive and kind of precocious child. I think sensitivity and intellect are closely linked because I easily noticed all the inequities in my life. Not having a father, raised by my grandmother, and my mother's mental illness was evidence of the haves vs. the have-nots. Bill Wilson said alcoholics are immature, oversensitive, and grandiose in his book, *The Twelve Steps and The Twelve Traditions*. I believe this is true, and perhaps my interpretation of getting the most out of the twelve steps, which have helped others as they are, is indeed a bit grandiose. I'd rather aim high and miss high than aim low and miss low. I'm not going to divulge too much about my childhood. In their conspiracy of silence, there are those I was raised by who'd rather I didn't. I'll touch on the dysfunction in a general way that leaves no doubt about what I dealt with.

To put it point-blank, I never felt like I fit in with life on earth. I wasn't succeeding very well in school and felt stupid, even though my IQ was pretty high. I didn't know how to fit among my schoolmates, as I was an only child raised primarily around adults. As I've mentioned, I first discovered food, then toys, and eventually reading to escape the feeling of not being loved or wanted. As a child, when we see this occurring, we quickly ask ourselves things like, "What is wrong with me that people keep leaving?" "Why didn't my father want me?" "Why is everyone so angry all the time?" and "How can I be happy?" These questions turned into blaming myself for the reasons these things occurred. I eventually discovered something that worked better than toys, books, and food to quell my discomfort. I hung out with the local hooligans, and they said, "Here, try drinking this," and "Try a hit of this joint." Low and behold, my ship had arrived. I was on a journey; the destination was unknown, and I didn't care.

I found my solution to all my dilemmas in substances. While substance abuse problems came rather quickly, it was a price I was willing to pay for the comfort it afforded me. The substances didn't start as a problem, but they came as a solution to my habitual problems in life. Drugs and alcohol didn't help me become a better student, a better son, a better member of society, better at sports, or anything. I simply didn't care as long as I had some liquor and marijuana. It should be noted that this took off rather quickly and in a very addictive manner. I remember my uncle leaving his marijuana out with his bong. He told me to help myself. He arrived home from work later and asked, "Where is all the pot?" I told him I smoked it all as he said I should "help myself." He hid his pot from that time forward. Smoking a quarter ounce should have been a warning sign for me but I was oblivious and mostly still happy to be so.

I continued to seek companions who, like me, enjoyed partaking in substances heavily. We hung out with an older crowd. I was still and would continue to stay emotionally immature throughout my period of substance use. I remember going out with my friend Tommy's friend Dave. Dave had a car, and we did not. Dave could get liquor, and the babes liked him. He had everything we thought we could ever desire. I remember Dave coming to pick us up. I hurriedly put away my GI Joe figures and hid them under my bed so my friends wouldn't think I was lame and set out for a night of drunken debauchery. This action illustrates where I was on a level of emotional maturity when I began my substance abuse. I've heard, and I believe it's true, that one stays emotionally stunted to where they are when they start abusing substances. My grades were suffering, my interpersonal relationships were terrible, and my family didn't offer much solid guidance to someone soon to be wrapped in substance abuse. This action was a recipe for disaster.

I somehow graduated from high school, and my substance use took off further and faster with employment. I worked at many restaurants, landscaping, factories, and anything to support the habit. It was the late nineteen eighties, and crack cocaine hit the scene. Not all of my friends hit the same path I did, but a few of us went deep. My best friend and I, along with four other friends, went down to the city searching for some marijuana. It was a dry summer, and not many of our local dealers had pot for us to purchase. It was late at night, and all the purveyors of the finest weed (Mexican brick pack) had retired for the evening. We found some fine young entrepreneurs selling the new improved Crack Cocaine. Of course, we thought it was a capital idea to purchase and give this a go. We didn't even have the proper equipment to smoke this substance. Crack is cocaine freed from its base, making it smokable in a particular type of pipe. We smoked it in a bowl designed to smoke marijuana. Of the six of us in the car, only Tommy and I actually ingested the cocaine vapor into our lungs. That was lucky for them because Tommy and I were hooked from the very start.

Crack is expensive, comparably so to marijuana and booze. We spent the next couple of years pursuing crack cocaine. Early in my foray into smoking cocaine and having very little money, a dealer got into the car with a few of us. He had a large quantity of crack on him. My drug-addled nineteen-year-old brain came across this thought, "If I hit him over the head with a rock, we could have all his crack to smoke." I somehow refrained from causing this man bodily damage or death to secure my evening entertainment. It was easy to see that this form of "entertainment" was going no place good. One of the last times I used cocaine, a street person stole my laptop, and I set after him with a large knife. I got into the middle of the street, and something just stopped me and told me to go home. I was headed to kill a man who had stolen a computer. We become different people in survival mode and under the obsession to use a drug.

The best description of the disease I've heard is that an addict doesn't know what will happen after the first drink or drug. Oftentimes, nothing terrible occurred; I'd just zone out and watch television wasted. Other times, I'd wind up in handcuffs, lose control of my bowels, and wreck everyone's evening with belligerent behavior or other travesties. The worst cases don't often happen to alcoholics because their drug is legal, socially acceptable, and cheap enough that they could panhandle for enough money to attain their ends. When you are in the grips of addiction, and the choice is between that drug you need and the value you were raised with, it's very easy to say, "Screw the value!"

Good people make terrible choices all the time. When I was training to bring meetings into the local prison, we had to take a class from the corrections officers on how to deal with the inmates. The training officer said most of the people incarcerated there for many years were of the "one bad night/decision" variety. They were living perhaps a precarious existence of materialism, drunkenness, and addiction, often under the influence when they made one bad choice. They now were paying for it— frequently for many, many years. I made many of the same bad choices these men did, but blessedly, I wasn't caught, or the circumstances weren't as bad. I needed to try to bring them recovery because they were me.

I eventually stumbled into my journey of going to treatment. I won't bore you with all the details of every foray into treatment I went through. I stumbled into 12 Steps fellowship through different attempts in these institutions. Did I use this fellowship as intended? The answer is a resounding "No!" Typically, I'd hand out and drink coffee, smoke cigarettes, and usually look down my nose at the people there. I generally thought, "Turning to God to solve their problems, what a bunch of grinning idiots." I'd compare my story to their stories and sit in judgment of them. I'd never been to prison. I never had a DUI. I'd never beaten a mate. I compared myself right out of the rooms. Eventually, much later on, I learned to identify with the feelings that brought these ladies and gentlemen into the fellowship. Those feelings of dread, isolation, disconnectedness, depression, anxiety, and despair were universally felt. I had felt the same. When I listened to how they felt, I identified with them, but this didn't happen for a great many years. It turned out it didn't matter what they were recovering from if I used the formula of identifying instead of comparing. Addictions are myriad, gambling, drugs, pornography, sex, alcohol, co-dependence, etcetera. When I listened to how they felt and stopped sitting in judgment, I started to see patterns.

After several stays in rehab and multiple failures, I eventually put together some sober time. You'll see that stringing sober days together isn't the same as recovery as we will delve into in this book. Some things did get better from just putting the substances away. I could hold a job because I wasn't calling in sick twice a week. I wasn't getting arrested because I wasn't breaking the law. I could have a relationship because I wasn't showing up after the first date drunk on their lawn, declaring my undying love for them. I spared many young ladies the misery of dating drunken Paul by doing so, though. During these eight years of dry in the fellowship, we call them "Dry Drunks," I thought I just needed to seek the right stuff to attain happiness. A dry drunk is one who stops imbibing substances, but never corrects the behavior for which they needed to use substances in the first place: anger, poor social skills, poor communication, low self-esteem, and fear to name those most prevalent. If I sought the American dream, I'd be good to go. I hung out in meetings for about a year and decided they were not for me because I didn't want to use drugs or drink. I figured I'd just seek my happiness and make my fortune, and eventually, everything would fall into place. I was wrong again. During this time, I met my wife. Somehow, she is still my wife today. Her name is Graca De Jesus, which is Portuguese for "the grace of Jesus." This name is indeed fitting as she and her faith eventually led me to change myself. She attained this name, being born as the tenth child in the late pregnancy of her parents. Neither she nor her mother was expected to live. I thank God she did live, as, without her, I don't know I'd have ever become who I am today.

We married, and I continued to chase those goals that would make me happy and successful. I'm an artist and went to school for it, eventually getting a degree and being accepted into one of the best art colleges in the country. I'm a musician and started playing small venues and recording original music. I went to the gym and got six-pack abs. I had a pretty good, albeit unfulfilling, job and made a decent income. I eventually achieved all those things I worked for, but I was always chasing, and never catching, happiness. Every time I achieved a goal, it felt hollow. If you make a list to fulfill your ego and fulfill it every day, the ego will just make you a longer list each day. I was emotionally immature, just as the big book said. With or without my booze, I was restless, irritable, and discontent. I still had all the problems I had when I discovered substances and without the program, I had none of the tools I needed to solve these problems. I simply switched addictions during this time to more prestigious and sometimes laudable goals and other addictions. I was spending money I didn't have, rampantly using pornography, exercise, food, and eventually, once again, the one I really wanted—substances that made me feel high.

I was diagnosed with Lyme disease, and it had been so many years since I'd abused substances my doctor thought it'd be okay to give me a light opiate for pain. I didn't go into this blind, nor did I remind the doctor of my stays at different drug rehabs. I was dying for anything to take me away from being me. The script began my dive back into active addiction for the next 18 years. I'd surface to sober air a few times, but without much success. I became addicted first to prescription pain killers and eventually saw the economic reasoning behind using heroin. The doctors dried up the supply I felt necessary to function. I could purchase these prescription drugs illegally on the streets, but the price was astronomical. For the cost of a four-hour high on illegal oxycontin, I could purchase four days' worth of heroin.

I switched to methadone and Suboxone eventually, I didn't know I could ever live free of substances, and these allowed me a modicum of normalcy, i.e.: putting dinner on the table, showing up for a job, not disappearing on a weekend drug run. I reasoned this was better as I wasn't emptying the bank accounts or disappearing from my now growing family. I thought at least my children had their basic needs met: food, clothing, and shelter. I had very poor modeling of what being a father meant. I've realized that the most significant thing I deprived them and myself of was emotional security. I never valued or loved myself, so how could I know depriving them of that was indeed a deprivation?

Through the course of Medically Assisted Treatment (MAT), my mental illness was running rampant. I believe MAT to be an effective tool in treatment if used correctly. I also believe it seldom is used correctly. My ADHD was out of control, and I was taking amphetamines to regulate it, followed by benzodiazepines to fall asleep. I eventually was depressed to the point I stopped proper hygiene and finally had Electro Convulsive Therapy (ECT) to treat it. The main problem was all the drugs I was still taking, prescribed or otherwise. I also suffered from complex Post Traumatic Stress Disorder (PTSD) and bipolar disorder. Because these diagnoses were made during periods of sobriety greater than six months, so I have no reason to believe they were inaccurate.

Today I take no prescriptions to deal with any of these issues. The titration and elimination were done cautiously, carefully, and under proper medical care. I don't recommend anyone to simply stop any medication they are taking. I think one needs to become a better advocate for themself and seek proper ethical doctors who will cooperate toward their wellness. I had many healthcare professionals who didn't fit this bill. They were the experts, and I was the novice, and that was that. I eventually became the expert, as I knew how I felt, and they could only speculate. To be fair, during this time, I was neither honest with myself nor with most of the healthcare professionals. However, I was given much erroneous information on the drugs prescribed, granted they only knew what the incomplete studies told them. I was told there wasn't any addiction to Suboxone or detox if I wanted to stop taking it. This was an outright lie. I was told that without Lithium, Depakote, or Lamictal, my bipolar disorder would be unmanageable, and I'd probably give in to suicidal ideations. While this is statistically correct, it isn't a complete assessment. I recently had a physical with my doctor, and the look on his face when I told him I wasn't taking any psychiatric medications was priceless. There was a lot I had to put into practice to achieve this level of wellness free of drugs. I changed my diet, exercise patterns, social life, thinking, communications, self-care, and more. Luckily, I could do it a little bit at a time, in bite-size chunks, one day at a time—taking it easy, easy does it but do it, and one day at a time. These little maxims AA has on their walls become very deep if you take the time to analyze them.

Between the years 2014 and 2018, my actual demise escalated. I was imprisoned during this time for carrying my prescription drugs unlabeled. I was detained in the Adult Correctional Institute (ACI) for two weeks. While the charges were blessedly dropped, confinement was a harrowing experience. I only knew of prison from what I watched on HBO and other television shows. I'm no tough guy, but I got on without having a fight because I'm intimidating to look at. I also kept my mouth shut and practiced good manners. It was boring and stressful. Plus, the food was awful, and some of the company was downright scary. Intake is not maximum security, but you are in intake if you are on trial. This means there were murderers, rapists, and other violent felons surrounding me. When I was released, many of my prescriptions were cut off because it was found out I had been abusing them once again.

I'd like to say that going to jail was enough for me to clean up my act, but I cannot.

I continued taking my MAT, and by 2017, I was suicidal. Graca had gone to Al-Anon during the years in between my different attempts at sobriety. Her knowledge of enabling received at Al-Anon eventually became a vehicle to exacerbate my eventual change. She did things like not letting me enter my home if I was intoxicated. She'd tell me I could sit in the car in the driveway until I was sober. I'd cause a fight, and say "I'm leaving," and she'd say if I did, she'd call the police to report me for driving intoxicated. She became the enemy of my self-destruction, and since it was all-encompassing, she was my enemy too.

I rediscovered the joy of using cocaine in 2016, and this was a vehicle for a fast ride to self-destruction, and also exacerbated my need for recovery toward trying once more to become sober. A family friend started taking me to AA meetings every week. I'd get a little bit of semi-sober time and relapse. My home life continued to deteriorate. From the summer of 2017 until May 9, 2018, I was in eight different hospitals. I had my first DUI and an earnest suicide attempt. I struggled and struggled but couldn't grasp sobriety. The family friend wasn't judgmental of me still taking the

Suboxone, but watching my repeated relapses, said he wasn't sure I'd get the spiritual nature of the program while still under the influence of this drug. He suggested that I think about getting off someday. I had to admit it didn't look promising the way things were going. The problem was I had tried to detox from Suboxone during one of my stays in a Rhode Island mental institution, drug rehab, and finally a center for co-occurring disorders in California. The results were that the last doctor called my wife and begged her to allow me to start taking it again as I'd lost all desire to live.

To sum things up, by the time I had gone to an addiction center in Laguna Beach, California, I was a scholar who couldn't comprehend language. I was a musician who hadn't played music in ten years. I was a trained artist who made no art. I was devoid and bankrupt in all areas of my life, a few being: mentally, spiritually, emotionally, financially, and physically. I didn't want to be sober, but my means to get high were methodically and systematically removed until I had no choice but to try sobriety again. I ceased to care for my own hygiene, and one counselor had to inform me I was the "stinky guy" in rehab. I was too low to feel much embarrassment by this time.

I was loaded onto a plane on May 9th, 2018. My wife was told they could humanely detox me from the drugs I'd been taking for a great many years. This wasn't entirely or even partially true. Granted, they tried to make it painless but failed. It should be noted that I was scheduled to fly out to California on the 8th but was too intoxicated to board the plane. My wife and my son tried cajoling the airline into taking me, but I was far too drunk to travel. I passed out walking down my driveway going back home, and while my son tried his best to catch me, dead weight is hard to support— and I was indeed dead weight.

The California sun was blinding and painful to my semi-intoxicated eyes when I arrived at the airport in Orange County. I was picked up by a man who held the same position I now hold in my current job. His name was Sean, and I believed he was plotting against me from the get-go. I can't tell you how grateful I became for Sean's help and honesty throughout my stay. I can't begin to express the gratitude I feel for being able to sit still in a chair or eat beef jerky today without losing a tooth. Little did I know

I wouldn't stop shaking for several months. Parkinsonism started once I stopped ingesting the drugs. Parkinsonism presents as the symptoms of Parkinson's disease without having the actual condition. It would be almost ten months before I started having a gait that wasn't shaky. I would experience weeks without any kind of sleep lasting more than minutes, being shipped to another psych facility after a suicide attempt in rehab. I was down to 135lbs at my lowest weight but would balloon up like crazy as my metabolism crashed.

I'm only writing about how bad my detox was because I'm assuming that by the time you can comprehend these words well enough to take action toward your recovery, you will have detoxed too. I don't tell people newly entering treatment how bad this was because it seems to vary from person to person, and I don't want my words to lead them toward a worse experience. The power of suggestion is strong. For example, I'll point out to my clients now, "Remember the feeling you got when the dealer said, 'Everything is all set, just come get it,' or when you purchased a bottle, and it sat on the car seat unopened just waiting to drink it? When I did that, I'd start feeling better almost immediately, knowing relief was on its way." The relief would occur before even ingesting the substance.

This is the power of hope.

This is the power of belief.

This is the power of our minds.

I provided a good amount of work for those treatment advocates in California. I had severe Post Traumatic Stress Disorder (PTSD), and when I did sleep, I was often found in weird locations. Sometimes I fell asleep under the bed, once in a closet, and once on top of the wardrobe in the room. I also slept with a plastic bag over my head, which got me shipped out and declared 5150, which is the California civil commitment code, and now I knew what that Van Halen album "5150" was talking about. Once again, thank you and kudos to those unsung heroes of the facility who met my insanity with kindness and mercy.

The sleep deprivation eventually led to vivid hallucinations, which were eventually discovered by staff. My delusions were discovered because though women were in their own unit in an all-male facility, I was entertaining a beautiful young lady in my room. I was providing moral support while she spoke with her father, who was half-man, half ceiling vent. Our entanglement was only discovered because at lunch, another client was making the moves on her, and I didn't like his intentions. I reported this to staff, and they asked when this client dissed my friend and me. I told them this had just occurred at lunch in the dining room. I was informed it was 10 am, and this didn't happen. The hallucinations might have been discovered earlier had I mentioned the ceiling vent man. Weird that even in hallucinations, we don't want to mention the wildly bizarre ones when they occur. While sleep was not forthcoming during the rehab stay, and no drugs they could prescribe could alleviate my symptoms, I simply started telling them I had no symptoms. At home, when I couldn't sleep, I could always rely on Netflix 24 hours a day. The facility turned off its television at 11 pm, and the next eight hours were spent pacing. I figured at least at home I'd be able to watch TV. I was at least honest by my exit assessment at the odds of me actually staying sober. It was a multiple-choice questionnaire, and one was least likely to stay sober, and ten was most likely to stay sober. I completed the questionnaire marking fives for every item down the list. I had been to something like 30 different programs and didn't hold out much hope for winning the recovery lottery.

It turns out there is no recovery lottery. There is a lot of work, dedication, learning, practice, prayer, meditation, and preparation. If I had known how much work there was to do, I would have declared. "What an order. I can't go through with it."

"Sobriety was the best gift I ever gave myself."

– Rob Lowe

CHAPTER TWO

Why Hacking the 12 Steps is Important

I'm writing this book because I've found happiness, joy, and equanimity through life's trials and tribulations. My mood is no longer based on what is happening and when. After years of major depression, bipolar disorder, PTSD, ADHD, and major anxiety, I no longer even need any medication to control these disorders. This wasn't easy, but it was doable—one day at a time.

I had to change everything to experience recovery, and through the years, I failed at succeeding in using the 12 Steps. My failures were, in large part, my own. I have a good intellect, and I believe addicts and alcoholics are generally above average in the IQ department. Having an above-average IQ nestled alongside a disorder such as addiction can be detrimental to getting help. We can argue the case to keep using substances often as well as or better than a famed attorney. I fooled many into believing I needed these substances or convinced them that my use of them was not a problem. I never succeeded in fooling myself, though I tried and tried. Having a high IQ is also a detriment because it allowed me to get by using a small percentage of my brain to function. In active addiction, especially in the beginning, I could put 25% of my mental faculties toward addiction and use the rest to function. I'd work my job or my relationship just good enough to not get fired or dumped. Addiction progressively takes more of our resources until it eventually hoards them all. I applied this get-by attitude toward my recovery when I started. I can now attribute many of my failures to just getting by. I'd get by until I didn't—and by didn't, I mean I drank or got high again, reigniting the fire of my obsession.

There were other factors that didn't help outside of my own laziness. Poor mentorship (sponsorship) in the fellowship, poor knowledge from those people, giant egos, often called bleeding deacons, and predators. Sadly, predatory behavior is particularly an issue for young women entering the program. Many "gentlemen" wish to offer women in the program a spiritual injection of the cock variety. When I entered the program while I was younger, in great shape, and better looking than I am today, I was prone to have the same mindset. These things can lead us away from this beautiful program. I was led away many times for many of these reasons until I was blessed with a good mentor who was humble enough to teach me what he knew and admit what he did not. I was quite the devil's advocate and skeptic of this process because of resentment toward what I'd seen religious people do in their hypocrisy.

I didn't believe for a minute this program would ever work for me. I didn't even have the most basic requirement for membership which is a desire to stop. I wanted to stay sober only more than I wanted to live on the street and those were my last two options—recovery or imminent demise on the streets. I also wanted to be able to look my now-adult children in the eyes and tell them I honestly did the best I could, and it didn't work. At least if I failed after exhausting this last option, I had done all I could. They could move on with their lives and just come to whatever acceptance they could about my fate. I also held onto the notion that if recovery through AA didn't work, I could always choose a more lethal approach to suicide and opt-out that way.

The suicide "solution" became a non-option after about four months sober. I had a loved one who took this route. He was as close to a brother as I had ever known in life, and he chose suicide as his way out. Though we had been estranged for many years, our paths were similar. When I started seeking treatment for my substance abuse, I was told I had to change the people I hung out with as well as the places I hung out. I'd heard it said before, "Change your playgrounds, playmates, and playthings." Though we had been apart for many years, and I was suffering extreme anhedonia from prolonged detox, I broke when I heard the news he had passed. Anhedonia is the inability to feel. We often think we use drugs and drink to get numb, yet absolute numbness is not enjoyable. During this numb period of post-acute withdrawal syndrome, I realized it wasn't the numbness I sought but the euphoria caused by using drugs and alcohol. If I had broken down upon hearing this news in my state of being, I knew those closer to him would never get over this loss. Suddenly it was clear that my idea that my wife and children would get over the suicide solution turned out to be another lie I told myself. Now my hope relied on this program working. If not, life would be a long, long trudge of white knuckle gripping tenuous sobriety until my final demise.

"To thine own self be true" is the mantra printed on the chips they hand out in meetings. I believe we have a still small voice inside us that will not allow us to align ourselves with bullshit. Some call this the conscience. I don't believe in coincidences. I think we all have a spark of energy in us that is of divine origin. That spark is a spirit, a soul, or the Ka as termed by the Egyptians. If we clear out things like fear, anger, discord, negative thought, and bad childhood programming obscuring this voice, it will tell us what we need to do. I'm sure you have heard the expression, "trust your gut." I believe we can align to what's true to our values by cleaning our body, mind, and spirit, and changing our ways to be in alignment with this spark which is sometimes referred to as intuition. A myriad of things kept me out of alignment: selfishness, entitlement, pride, anger, lust, gluttony, etcetera. These are things we will look at further in later chapters on the steps.

This book isn't written to be done in place of the 12 Steps. I'm writing this to augment the process. There are processes within the 12 Steps that I haven't seen applied much in the program, but they have all come from its practice. Many skimp on many things laid out and don't get the full application. I can't even say I've seen the full application of these steps, as they are a daily practice and will continue to improve over a lifetime with practice. This book is merely support to help you navigate what is known as the program and the fellowship. The program is the 12 Steps themselves, while the fellowship is meetings and people sharing their individual experiences, strength, and hope.

I hope this guide will help you recover as it has done for me.

The program and fellowship gave me hope when I was hopeless, gave me meaning when life was meaningless and made my life what it is today: full, thriving, happy, and filled with joy.

"Accept failure. Enjoy it even.
Embrace the suck, for the suck is part of the process,"

—AJ Jacobs

CHAPTER THREE

Embracing the Suck

I work with a lot of veterans, and one adage I've picked up from them is the idea of embracing the suck. To me, embracing the suck means getting through the awful parts to achieve a better end. These men and women go through grueling training and testing to achieve their goals. They are pushed beyond their limits to achieve what they once saw as impossible. Their bodies and minds are tested as they have never been tested before. When they succeed, they become something different from the person they were initially. They become soldiers, Marines, Navy Seals, and Special Forces. They have a sense of pride in their accomplishment, yet most I've met still have humility. They credit their instructors, their family, and their country.

I've seen a meme on social media that says a lot. It says, "Marriage is hard, divorce is hard, working out is hard, obesity is hard. Choose your hard." Hard is indeed true for recovery. Early recovery for me was a constant battle with my own mind. I had pervasive thoughts of drinking, suicide, and other intrusive and uncomfortable thoughts. I found out a lot of my depression was caused by these thoughts. When I could look into what I thought while I was depressed, after I had gained a little bit of clarity, I could see this. When depressed, I thought, "Life sucks." "I'm a loser." "I failed before; why would I succeed now?" "My wife is going to leave me." "I'm going to die alone penniless and on the streets or in prison." I could see why I was so depressed when looking at these thoughts. The thalamus, the part of the brain that addresses sensory input, attaches emotion to every thought we have, and negative thoughts invite negative emotions.

In the beginning, I had to do whatever I could to make these destructive thoughts go away. Prescription medicine worked for a period, clouded my head, and eventually stopped having any effectiveness. That was when I started to pray. I didn't know who or what I was praying to; I simply would shout in my head, "Please make this stop!" It wasn't fun thinking about how great a trip to the liquor store would be if I wasn't going to do it. If you're uncomfortable praying to a higher power and it helps you think of prayer as simply a mantra to your subconscious mind, do that. A prayer or mantra is a request that you cooperate with yourself and stop having pervasive thoughts. Talking to other people was also a big help to me. At the beginning of most meetings, they will usually ask for a show of hands of anyone new or coming back. This isn't to embarrass you. It's to show the individuals who could use some help. It can be embarrassing to ask, but it's worthwhile to start acquiring some phone numbers of sober people you can turn to for help. As hard as it is to ask another for help, don't feel like you are being a bother. Helping others in their times of need is part of Step 12, and I get as much if not more out of being there for someone new than they ever do from me. I've found it helps to just start out texting some of these individuals to start a little dialogue. This way when my ass is on fire, and I call in the middle of the night because the obsession is in full bloom, I've already had some contact. I answer the phone day or night when I know someone needs me. Many times, someone else's problems come just in time to help me out. Maybe I need to follow the advice I dispense to them, and perhaps I'm sitting around in my own self-pity, thinking nobody cares about poor Paul. Somehow, listening to another person's problems works to magically make me forget about my own. The paradox of love is that the more I give, the more I receive, the more valued I feel, and the more worthwhile my purpose feels.

Eventually, the obsessive thoughts were removed through replacement with prayers, mantras, health activities, and self-care. Harmful thoughts were replaced with little thoughts of gratitude and thanks. I'd say things like, "I'm living and sleeping indoors today, thank you!" "I'm eating food from a refrigerator and not a rubbish bin, thank you!" "Hey, my legs stopped shaking enough to sit in a chair for an hour, thank you!" "Wow, I can eat a candy apple again without losing a tooth, thank you!" The list of

Paul Moore

gratitude and thanks could go on ad infinitum for me today. If I'm starting to dwell in negativity, I talk/pray my way out of it. I'd do this by saying things like, "The rest of the day is going to get better," and maybe I throw a please and a thank you to my higher power at this request. These negative thoughts started to wind down as I began to do a little work in the steps. If I was actually reading them or asking questions about them, I felt like I was at the very least doing something.

There is something to be said for being grateful for what you have instead of looking at what is missing from your life. I've found this principle can even be applied to terrible situations. Even when something as harrowing as "My wife is divorcing me" can become "Maybe I'll find someone who loves me more who I love more." I started thinking, "Why not me? I'm not the stupidest, the least talented, or the ugliest. Why not me?" I started projecting, "My day will be great," through my mental field, actions, and thoughts. When the woman at the convenience store asked, "How are you?" I'd reply, "Fantastic!" I eventually even started meaning it and feeling fantastic. I fooled myself with my words.

The practice of gratitude should, like everything in your recovery, be as honest as possible. There are things other people may suggest as possible and something you should be grateful for. If you are not grateful for these things, don't say you are. I might be grateful for having my children, but if they were behaving like spoiled little ingrates all day, I certainly don't feel grateful for that. Write down things you are really grateful for, even if it's a minuscule thing or amount. While I wasn't happy that my wife didn't let me coast on a chemical cloud unto my death because I didn't want to be sober at that time, I was grateful that my wife was still willing to support me.

Take some time to list a few things you are actually grateful for and give thanks.

_____

_____

_____

_____

_____

_____

_____

_____

_____

_____

Take some time to list a few things you are actually grateful for and give thanks.

_____

_____

_____

_____

_____

_____

_____

_____

_____

_____

Faith Gratitude List

This chapter is based on something I've been noticing more recently. It's reminiscent of the Janet Jackson song, "What have you done for me lately?" It's very easy to return to a negative when I've been wronged, treated unjustly, angered, or am experiencing any discomfort. That is just how easy it is to forget just how much my higher power has delivered me through, especially when I'm having a bad day. When I'm in these states of doubt, there are many things I can do to break out of them. Having a list of just what I've survived and been delivered from has been helpful to me. I suggest perhaps keeping this list on you. It can be copied to your phone or another device. This survival and deliverance list should not take the place of a daily gratitude list if you are in the habit of making one. This list should come across as a life gratitude list, and I'll put mine down as an example.

It's off the top of my head and far from a complete listing, but here is a list of things my higher power has delivered me from.

- I've been delivered from and survived: a dysfunctional childhood and trauma.
- I've been delivered from and survived: constant bullying for many years.
- I've been delivered from and survived: countless near misses with death, from overdoses to driving under the influence, to dangerous drug transactions, and more.
- I've been delivered from and survived: mental illness.
- I've been delivered from and survived: drug addiction.
- I've been delivered from and survived: prison.
- I've been delivered from and survived: homelessness.
- I've been delivered from and survived: my family hating me.
- I've been delivered from and survived: poor health.
- I've been delivered from and survived: bad jobs.
- I've been delivered from and survived: endless depression and melancholy.
- I've been delivered from and survived: attempted suicide.

I think you are getting the gist of this exercise. Make a list for your own use.

I've left space for you.

I've been delivered from and survived:

_____

_____

_____

I've been delivered from and survived:

_____

_____

_____

I've been delivered from and survived:

_____

_____

_____

I've been delivered from and survived:

_____

_____

_____

I've been delivered from and survived:

_____

_____

_____

I've been delivered from and survived:

_____

_____

_____

I've been delivered from and survived:

_____

_____

_____

I've been delivered from and survived:

_____

_____

_____

I've been delivered from and survived:

_____

_____

_____

I've been delivered from and survived:

_____

_____

_____

I've been delivered from and survived:

_____

_____

_____

I've been delivered from and survived:

_____

_____

_____

Paul Moore

It's easy to look at what we've experienced as a higher power as a big mean bully on the playground. When we think this way, it's done from the perspective of want and have not. Unfortunately, this perspective will keep anyone a victim forever. Thoughts like, "If you grew up without a dad, you'd drink too," "If you had my mental illness, you'd do the same as me," and "If you suffered abuse, you'd overeat as well," are typical of statements made by those in a victim state. These statements are manipulative. I used statements like these to make people feel sorry for me and steer the discussion away from any subject I didn't want to discuss. Hey, when it worked, I could go back to vegetating in front of the television, imbibing my favorite substance.

Changing my perspective was fantastic for my self-esteem. I learned that the manipulative statements I used to get others to feel sorry for me and to leave me to the addiction could be flipped around. I may not have had my dad around, but God made sure some good male influences spent time with me. I have a mental illness, but I've learned techniques and changes in my lifestyle that not only make it tolerable but actually give me a unique mindset and interesting character. The abuse I suffered I survived, and now I'm a beacon to advocate against this sort of behavior, showing future generations they are not alone and helping to correct the problem.

I survived it all to tell my tale and write this book.

A quick google search will confirm that optimists live longer than pessimists, and optimists recover from illnesses, even serious ones like cancer, at a higher rate than those who are pessimistic. Optimists are generally happier and more satisfied with their lives. And just like pessimism, optimism is a learned and practiced behavior. You are not born an optimist nor a pessimist. These behaviors and thoughts are learned from others. When I spent time with my mother growing up, it was a nonstop complaint fest. Everyone had better than us, and everyone had what we deserved. She never got promotions because the other people wore a low-cut blouse or slept their way to the top. The list of her excuses and rationale for being a victim was endless, and I adapted the techniques she demonstrated to my own life.

I'd always make whatever problems I had even worse with this downtrodden attitude. Since I deluded myself by saying things like, "They got the job over me from being a kiss ass," I abdicated any and all responsibility on my part to achieve what I wanted. They may well have gotten the job from being a butt-kisser, but my thought didn't help me one bit. Maybe if I looked at my own inadequacies, I'd have found a complete answer as to why I didn't get the job. I likely didn't get the job because of the times I was late or hungover and the times I told my boss exactly what I thought of them. Even if these were not factors, by addressing my own issues, l could improve my performance at work. Plus, if it's true they only promote "yes men" toadies to better positions, maybe I had better change my employment.

The keynote of this, like all other aspects of recovery, is practice. Through recovery, we are consistently practicing mindfulness, practicing virtue, practicing changing negative thoughts, practicing going to meetings, practicing selflessness, and practicing prayer. Practice is indeed the key to a changed life. Early recovery is tenuous and hard to grasp, and the problems outweigh the solution on a regular basis. Constant support and the alleviation of stress are integral for prolonged and enduring change.

Instead of asking, "Why does nothing go right?" get in the practice of saying, "Well, this too shall pass," and "What else have I gotten through with help?" Instead of making excuses, practice asking. "What can I do to improve this situation?"

Instead of looking at the downside, try a gratitude meditation. Write down five or ten things that make you happy, and simply dwell on these things while breathing deeply into your gut.

Instead of reacting impulsively and thinking, "I must charge that new iPhone and have to stress later about the payments," perhaps sit and ask, "How much do I really need this, and what am I willing to sacrifice so I can make stress free payments?"

Paul Moore

"Sometimes you can only find Heaven by slowly backing away from Hell."

— Carrie Fisher

CHAPTER FOUR

Self-Care Isn't Selfish

Self-care isn't selfish. In fact, the more loving we are to ourselves, the more loving we can be to others who need our love. I've heard a metaphor describing a flight attendant telling passengers, "If the oxygen masks come down, you need to put yours on first, even before your loved ones. If you pass out, how can you help those you care about?" The problem is when we are new to recovery, more often than not, we have been behaving very selfishly in our addiction. Now, those we neglected along the way will have to wait longer for our love and support while we practice self-care. If unsure whether or not you should put yourself first, I can assure you that the answer is always "Yes." Self-care is one of the best ways to alleviate stress, especially in early sobriety. We must learn to cope without using a mind-altering substance, and stress will lead us back to addictions very quickly. It will not always be so, but in the beginning, it is absolutely necessary to sustain sobriety. Sustenance will give you a fighting chance to get to a level of equanimity and peace of mind that's not dependent on the gifts and problems life throws at us.

In early recovery, I had a plan where I could "tap out" of stress. Tapping out is akin to a self-care plan for when the shit hits the fan and the stress is too much. Like MMA, fighters can end the fight with a tap-out, meaning they concede to their opponent. It didn't take much stress initially for me to need to tap out. I remember not getting along well with my adult son in early recovery one day. The house was tense, and he stomped around, slamming cupboards, making for an unpleasant vibe in the house. I came home from caring for my mother-in-law, and the refrigerator was broken. Today, working, having some money saved, I'd simply order a new refrigerator. It was a different story back then. I was not working, short on money, and stressed from my son's irritation. The situation was more than I could handle. I tapped out. I talked to my sponsor and pissed and moaned for a while. Next, I went to my room and prayed for strength and a solution, opened a carton of soothing Ben and Jerry's strawberry cheesecake ice cream, grabbed my best friend, Sir Chremesickle, a large orange cat, turned on "The Office," and binge-watched until I fell asleep. It was a successful day sober! There are levels to this shit and back then a binge and a nap was a win.

The next day, the problem turned out not to be insurmountable. My wife called a second-hand place and found a new refrigerator we could afford to replace the one that crapped out. I didn't use drugs or drink—even through what I considered dire stress. Today, I handle problems that dwarf the refrigerator incident and don't get very stressed. Every once in a while, though, I still need to tap out and take care of myself in a big way. Most of the time, though, it's the culmination of many small practices that suffice to keep me at an even keel on a day-to-day basis.

Having a healthy routine is good self-care. What did my days look like, especially in early recovery? Frequently attending meetings was a good start. Talking to other people in recovery and setting up a solid support network of sober friends helped too. I'd go to work, go home, have dinner, grab a coffee, go to a meeting or counseling, and return home for some reading or television. I also made fun, sober plans for the weekend. In early recovery, plans are often dictated to us by health care professionals, the legal system, our employers, and our families. We still need to be our own best advocates to evaluate and pursue what is doable for us.

Keeping stress down requires some work as well. I indulged in a self-care day a couple of weeks ago. I had some pastry from a great bakery, a comfortable blanket, a great book, planned out some shows I wanted to see on television, and went to a meeting to start my day. Before beginning my day of indulgence, I washed the dishes, started my laundry, was in a routine of exercising regularly, and paid my bills with steady work. I wouldn't exactly be comfortable stuffing my face watching television if I had a bunch of daily worries going through my mind. My daily responsibilities needed to be handled to the best of my ability before I could truly enjoy my day. This doesn't mean you cannot have some self-care time if you are unemployed or have pending issues on the horizon. Even doing little baby steps of what you can, taking even five minutes out of your busy day to mindfully eat dark chocolate, or watch the sunset can be the difference between a good or bad day and is often enough to alleviate the anxiety. Perhaps I'd go online and fill out an application or two before taking the day off if I didn't have a job. If it was a legal issue, as I was still dealing with the aftermath of a DUI in early sobriety, perhaps I'd do one thing toward alleviating that problem.

I've found that doing something and taking action is a good cure for anxiety. Usually, the action is not as bad as my imagining how bad the action will be. I hated and still hate mowing the lawn. I would think about the grass growing every day. I'd think about how long it took to mow, how many rocks I'd need to avoid, how sweaty I'd get in the hot sun, and then I'd dwell on these thoughts about the lawn every day until I finally mowed it. It takes a bit over an hour to care for my lawn once per week. Yet, I'd spend countless hours dwelling on how terrible it would be. I made a plan to alleviate my lawn stress. I decided I'd mow the lawn every Friday in the morning after I awakened and had my coffee. This plan did a couple of things. First, I'd get the task out of the way before the day's heat became unbearable. Second, I'd do it early before I dwelled on the terribleness of the chore. Once mowing the lawn, I stopped thinking about how much more I had to do and attentively focused on making one perfect row.

One decision and action plan stopped me from worrying about how terrible it would be all week long. I knew I didn't have to mow the lawn until Friday. Suddenly, I was freed from days of thinking about just how terrible mowing the lawn would be. Mindfully mowing the lawn wasn't so bad, and focusing my intent on the perfect row cleared me of thinking of how much was left. I still don't enjoy the chore of mowing the lawn, and now that I'm working at a job, I can even pay someone else to do this onerous chore for me. These same adulting strategies and skills can be employed for alleviation of much daily stress. We can set reminders for paying our bills. Find more economical ways to entertain ourselves to avoid debt. A nice hike in the woods costs perhaps gas money, a picnic we make ourselves is doing self-care, and if we share it with another, it becomes service. If I'm stressed from the highway ride to work and the traffic, I can endeavor to leave a bit early and perhaps have a good playlist or audiobook to enjoy my ride better.

Try to come up with some of your own strategies to alleviate the stress of your life. Each suggestion should be doable and not overwhelming. When I was still suffering hard from depression, some days, my only goal would be to move from the bed to the sofa to watch television. At least that way, I accomplished one thing.

Lists can also be a big help. In the beginning, I liked to start lists with some things I had already accomplished to build the momentum of accomplishment. Here's a typical list for me early in recovery:

- ✓ Wake up, check.

- ✓ Make bed, check.

- ✓ Brush teeth, check.

- ✓ Make coffee, check.

- Go to court.

- Go to the department of motor vehicles.

- Wash dishes.

- Do laundry.

- Pay phone bill.

If lists like this seem like a lot of work, remember the AA adage, "Easy does it." My sponsor would add, "but do it," to this adage. "Easy does it, but do it." His upgrade of the phrase offered the necessary action component that gave me a sense of accomplishment. My days now are full. I often work seven days a week toward my eventual goal of opening a sober living facility for treatment-resistant addicts suffering from a co-occurring disorder. I write every day. I do my best to spend hours volunteering service in the fellowship several times per week. I meditate every day and practice keeping my dreams in sight many times a day. In my spare time, I've gotten my own facility certified with a partner. I still eat with my wife and try to have at least one date night every week or two. I text my children and friends in the fellowship on a daily basis. I take stock of my behavior every day and apologize and commit to change if it's not in line with my ideals. This may sound like a lot. But remember, I started some days by just moving from the bed to the sofa and picked up momentum a little at a time.

I've left space for you to brainstorm your self-care strategies and healthy daily plans. Make notes to describe your self-care plan.

_____

_____

_____

_____

_____

_____

_____

_____

_____

_____

_____

_____

_____

_____

_____

_____

_____

_____

_____

_____

_____

_____

_____

_____

_____

Random acts of kindness for their own sake

Part of my self-care regimen, and incorporated into Step 12, is a process of random acts of kindness and service to my fellow man without considering compensation or anyone giving me anything back.

Step 12 says, "Having had a spiritual awakening as the result of these steps, we tried to carry this message to alcoholics and to practice these principles in all our affairs."

I just realized, and I don't like to brag about this, that the money I earned during the last six weeks of the 2021 holiday season was given away, either in gifts, donations, "loans," or little acts of kindness spewed out across many different people. I put loans in quotations because it's up to the recipient whether they pay me back or not. Because I trust and love the individuals I loaned money to, I'll never ask them about whatever money they needed, nor did I even really inquire how they'd use it. I often get a stipend for being called into work above my overtime wage. I'd always use part of this to purchase pastry or meals for my co-workers.

Here's a side note and life hack for you. Chocolate makes all humans better after ingesting it. Even assholes become more tolerable after they eat a little chocolate. This little piece of magic superfood does wonders for the disposition.

Using the stipend to help my co-workers with a better mood made my overtime experience more enjoyable, and I gave credit to my work as they provided me with the extra money to purchase the goodies. While others complained that our employer should do more, I was grateful there was work to take care of my daily needs. It's funny, I was happier, and they were more miserable, though we both received the same stipend.

Before my vacation, I was cashing several checks at the bank that issued them, and they charged me $8 per check to cash. I guess Bank of America could learn a little about random acts of service. I took the money in large bills for an upcoming vacation with my wife. When leaving, there was a homeless woman standing at the intersection. My intuition told me to make her day and give her one of these large bills. I've learned to follow my intuition as of late and did just that, needing even to switch lanes to do it. She blessed me, and I don't even think she realized the bill's denomination. While some would say I was enabling an alcoholic or drug addict to continue using, I don't see it that way.

Here's how I see it. Perhaps this little display of human love and kindness might make the difference in that person choosing to get well in an unkind world. Frequently homeless people are avoided by even our eye contact, as they humble themselves to beg for what they need to get by. When I was addicted to drugs, I thought drugs were the only thing stopping me from suicide. In all honesty, they probably were, until I became suicidal even with the substances. Maybe next time I see a person I've blessed, they will ask me why I gave so much, and perhaps that will open the door for them to get some help.

The act of doing kindness to humanity at large is the second part of this step, "And to practice these principles in all our affairs." Many people get hung up on just carrying the message to other alcoholics and miss out on the healing practice of doing random acts of kindness throughout their daily lives. It took me a solid ten months to complete a thorough step process the first time. But these things I could practice almost from day one: gratitude for what I was truly grateful for, random acts of kindness, and some simple healthy self-care.

I remember about two years sober, and I was starting my internship and training for my peer recovery certification. I walked into a local Cumberland Farms convenience store for my morning coffee. It was one extravagance I afforded. In my early recovery, we were very financially strapped as my wife was our sole provider. We were very frugal during this period, but I still was able to get my affordable, delicious coffee as Cumberland Farms kept the price very low and reasonable. When I went to pay for this coffee, the person behind the counter told me, "No charge. The last customer bought the next fifty or so coffees!" I was thrilled by this surprise, it really made my morning, and I'll never forget that stranger's random act of kindness.

Due to mirror neurons that cause the same reaction in the brain when an individual produces or observes a behavior, this act of kindness was felt some 102 times that day. Forgive me if my math is off. When he did this, he and the clerk felt his sharing of love. Then every time the clerk told a customer, "Your coffee is paid for," the clerk and customer got to feel this anew and fresh. That's a serious number of endorphins and good energy shared among many individuals for a reasonably small price.

I'd like to mention I was able to get my license back and afford insurance due to a family member who'd like to remain anonymous. He provided me a loan of several thousand dollars to get my training and pay my fines for losing my license. The money was given as a loan. Upon starting working, I intended to pay this back before any extravagance for myself. We sent the first check of $500 as I planned the $5000 to be paid back in under a year with interest. I received a call when my relative received the first check. He said he wouldn't be cashing my checks to return the money and that it was a gift. I'm crying now as I write this because the value and love they placed on me, my worth, and my value are still quite poignant and touching to me to this day. I decided I'd pay them back in one way or another, as they wouldn't take remuneration from me, I've donated $500 in their names each year. I'll continue to do so at least until I've donated $5000. It feels so good I'll probably keep donating long after the $5000 is disbursed.

My first form of doing something for others was becoming my wife's personal chef. I'm a pretty good cook. Because we were low on money, we didn't buy many preprocessed foods. It was simply cheaper to cook food from scratch, and it turns out this was an added blessing as it is better for us too. She'd come home from work and ask, "What's for supper?" I'd simply answer, "Whatever you'd like me to make for you." This made me feel like I was just leeching off of her goodwill. Once I was back on my feet financially, my wife's plan was to divorce me. I was doing this anyway because she was still kind enough to help me recover and provide a roof over my head, for which I was quite grateful, having lived outdoors for a period of time.

While the examples I mentioned require some money, true random acts of kindness do not require any money. I can value someone's time by listening to their tale of woe. I can bring the extra food I cook from a meal to a loved one. I can hold a door open for someone too far to hold the door and not give them a sarcastic "You're welcome" when they forget to thank me. I can return someone's cart to the cart bin when they neglected to do it.

To get started, write some examples of random acts of kindness you can try throughout your day, also any you have done. These little esteemed acts will increase your feeling of value within yourself. Try to do it without expecting compliments, accolades, or recognition in return. I'm sure you will get some anyway, but try not to expect it. I've heard expectations described as premeditated resentments and have seen the truth in that.

_____

_____

_____

_____

_____

_____

_____

_____

_____

_____

_____

_____

_____

_____

_____

_____

_____

_____

_____

"The greatest mistake to make in life is to continually be afraid, you will make one."

—Elbert Hubbard

CHAPTER FIVE

12 Step Faux Pas

This chapter springs from a group I teach on 12 step breaches of etiquette. As a New Englander, I imagine these will vary based on locations and different meeting temperaments around the world. These are some I've encountered. My aim is to give you the best experience with the 12 Steps I can; some of these are unwritten rules that most people try to follow. Being unwritten, many newcomers break them without realizing, and some crotchety intolerant member often points them out. This can cause embarrassment, anger, and resentment and make one never want to come back. I've had many of these happen to me personally, and sometimes they took me away from the fellowship. I was always driven back under the lash of alcoholism and addiction. The need for a solution outweighed my embarrassment and anger.

Crosstalk

Often many of us have the experience in treatment or group therapy of interjecting while a person is speaking. While many of us get a lot out of sharing what we are going through, the 12 Steps aren't group therapy. It's a spiritual program and fellowship designed to solve your problems with addiction. I've found in speaker meetings, which are popular in my area, a group comes into another group, and members take turns sharing their experiences, strength, and hope. In these meetings, there is no raising your hand and speaking. In discussion meetings, a speaker usually shares for ten or fifteen minutes and opens the meetings for discussion with or without a topic. Some meetings are much more tolerant over the topics, and you'll have to evaluate the temperature of the meeting to know what's appropriate to discuss. I wouldn't suggest you walk into a meeting for the first time and drop your life's history, but if you've been going for a while, heard other people sharing similar experiences, and feel comfortable in the meeting, I'd say go for it. The fellowship is a room full of sick people working on getting well, and not everyone is at the same stage of the game.

Commenting directly on what someone shared is referred to as crosstalk. Now you'll see variations that don't raise anyone's anger. If someone shares and I speak of how I related to their story and it has many similarities to my own, no one will consider that crosstalk. If I offer criticism of how they are working the steps, living their lives, or acting, especially in front of the whole group, that will be considered crosstalk. Sometimes people cross-talk covertly. They could hop on something you've said and mention how wrong they find this in a non-direct way. Try to remember we are not looking toward those who are still intolerant and judgmental for guidance and practice the adage, "live and let live." This simply means I take what is good and leave the rest behind. I'm, after all, trying to reach a level of equanimity where people comment and life's problems don't change my overall mood or perception of myself. I'm trying not to take it personally.

There will be those who try to guide you toward their conception of God (Higher Power) in both loving and not-so-loving ways. A common or shared meaning of a Higher Power is nowhere in the literature. Your conception of your higher power is personal and indeed your own. Sometimes people may suggest it be loving and forgiving. This isn't a bad idea, as an indifferent higher power is one I had all my life and didn't work out so well. A good way to seek a loving Higher Power comes through prayer and especially meditation.

"Be still and know that I am God" comes to mind. In the quiet recesses of my mind, where I'm breathing deeply into my gut, and all the physical sensations fall away, is where I experience God the most. It's been said praying is asking, and meditation is receiving guidance. Prayer alone can be selfish and self-serving, whereas meditation is waiting for answers, which usually come in the sense of feeling what's right while we practice being more honest. If you make the ocean, a rock, Buddha, Allah, Krishna, or Jesus Christ your Higher Power, that is completely up to you. Some call God an acronym of Good Orderly Direction or Group Of Drunks. Your conception is your own.

Identify or relate rather than directly compare

I first went into the fellowship when I was very young. I heard tales of woe and horror that didn't apply to me at that time. I heard people who had been imprisoned for their drinking and drugs. I heard people who lived their lives on the streets because of their addiction. I heard tales of those with great homes and extravagant wealth. I heard people who used street drugs which are illegal. I've heard of those who only used alcohol or prescription drugs. When I compared at that young age, I compared myself right back into active addiction. I said things like, "I've never been to prison," and I should have added a "yet" to that statement. The malady of addiction is progressive and eventually led me to all those comparisons that didn't happen yet. The prevailing thought when I compared was, "Maybe I'm not that bad, maybe I'm not really an addict." It took years of trial and error to discover I indeed had an unmanageable life due to addiction.

If I listened to what the people felt when they were speaking, it didn't even matter if I was at a meeting that didn't apply to me, like Overeaters Anonymous or Gamblers Anonymous. Those feelings of isolation, loneliness, depression, despair, anxiety, and so forth are universal whether you use them on Park Avenue or the park bench. When my attitude was shifted to the right place and away from petty judgments, I could learn something from everyone. If it doesn't apply to you, it may just be one of those "yets." You too are eligible for if you continue your addiction.

Connecting with Sponsors

When it comes to connecting with sponsors, it's good to have men with men and women with women. This will be covered more in my chapter on choosing a mentor and twelve-step fellowships called these mentors sponsors. When these steps were written, they didn't address some modern issues. Actually, they didn't really have sponsorship, so to speak, in the early fellowship. A generally good rule of thumb is to have a sponsor where there is zero potential for sexual attraction either way. This, for many, is the first attempt at a wholly honest relationship with another human being. Getting really honest is difficult, and when you think there may be a chance of sleeping with your sponsor, it makes it even more difficult to talk about some of your more selfish acts—especially in the sexual arena.

Frequency of meetings

Ninety in ninety is a good rule of thumb for starting the meeting process. By committing in this way, you'll get to encounter many people, get phone numbers, and find the meeting where you feel the most comfortable. This will also keep you in the middle of the herd, so to speak. We don't often like to talk about relapse in the business of recovery because it's a sore subject and makes people feel like failures. But if you are going to meetings every day or at least quite often, a slip of using might be a weekend of despair instead of a full return to active addiction. When attending regularly, you are more likely to say, "Wow, that sucked. They were right, and maybe I should return and evaluate where my recovery was weak," instead of "Damn, I messed up, I guess recovery isn't for me."

The above guidelines are certainly not a complete list of the etiquette that could be broken. They're just some of the more glaring ones I have encountered personally. Don't let anyone drive you away from your recovery. You have as much a right to be there as the person with 30 years sober. Be your own best advocate.

"It is one of the most beautiful compensations of this life, that no man can sincerely try to help another without helping himself."

—Ralph Waldo Emerson

CHAPTER SIX

Finding Proper Mentorship (Sponsoring)

Sometimes the perfect sponsor will just fall into your lap as if magically, and sometimes you'll need to be observant and look diligently for the proper connection. The truth was, I didn't know how to be happy, and therefore I didn't even know what to look for. Blessedly, a family friend started picking me up and taking me to meetings. He was very into the twelve steps and believed they held the answer to my dilemmas. He still picked me up for meetings in thick and thin, and even through my many relapses, he was steadfast. He was also quite devout to his religion and quite humble. He never pushed his religion on me and one of the most telling things about his character was his lack of anger, even when I'd criticize his beliefs.

He was by no means perfect, but he was genuine and humble. When he didn't have an answer, he didn't get mad and tell me to do as he said anyway. I'm the devil's advocate by nature and question everything. So, whenever there was something that didn't seem like it would work, in my opinion, I questioned it. When he told me prayer helped him in his recovery, I scoffed at the idea. I figured that if he knew my life, he knew any God didn't really give a crap about me. I had gone over the history of atheism and all the scholarly atheist arguments of the enlightenment period and could argue against God all day long. He out common sensed me, though, and defeated all my arguments with one question. He simply asked, "How is it going to hurt you to try this?" When I replied arrogantly, "You're telling me I'm going to ask Santa Clause in the sky for favors?" he simply laughed. Most Christians I knew up to this time would have become angry, resentful, and irritable given my criticism of their beliefs. He did not.

I still didn't trust anyone, including him, very much. I was pretty shut down, and my experience in trust was if I trusted someone, I could expect to be betrayed. I opened the door to trust and honesty rather slowly. I had a weekend relapse during our time of going to meetings, and my wife didn't catch me. Considering my mentor was a family friend, I thought the news of my relapse might get back to my family if I told him, but I told him anyway. My being caught by my family was of no use to anyone, and it would only hurt and worry them having this knowledge. In Step 9, I had read we make amends except in cases when doing so would hurt others. I thought this truth to tell him was a prime example of a situation like this, and by telling him, I could determine his trustworthiness. After I shared the secret with him, I wasn't caught, he didn't feel the need to broadcast what happened, and trust between us began to develop.

He also still had problems that made him more relatable to me. His life wasn't going perfectly, but he still wasn't taking substances. This was mystifying to me. He had gained some stability, and his problems were not leading him back to his former solution, which was booze. Sometimes in the fellowship, people get to the point where they act like they've become the second coming of Christ. They never speak of any problems they still encounter. At least from the outside, it appears they have the perfect sobriety and recovery. They are ready to perform miracles; they have reached the "cool kid" phase of recovery. I've found people like this are usually full of shit. Being a cool kid feels great, and I've had to make sure I don't dwell in this phase myself. I work in rehab with newly recovering people, and they like to put me on this pedestal at times. Because knowing others think highly of me strokes my ego and makes me feel good, I can see why people get stuck being a cool kid, thinking their shit doesn't stink. It's like being the popular quarterback in high school. Beware, this is not relatable or realistic. While one can get to the point where the problems easily roll off their backs, life still sends trials. How we deal with them can almost seem magical to someone, like I was at the time, unfamiliar with how this works.

Side note: How it works is on page forty-eight of the book Alcoholics Anonymous.

I tested my mentor's trust quite a few more times before I was ready to purge my behavior, which comes in steps four and five. I never had any other fellows in the meeting asking awkward questions about my needing Viagra at the time or anything else I told him privately. I can easily talk about most of these embarrassing things now because I work the steps.

As I've spoken on earlier, when I arrived at my first meeting, I was unemployable, bankrupt, and not even really keeping up with my personal hygiene. My teeth were rotting, my metabolism crashed, and I was quite fat. He had quite a challenge taking me through this process. My sponsor was far from perfect in his guidance on lots of things too. I've heard if your marriage is suffering or your back is aching; you should probably take those things to their proper places; being a marriage counselor or maybe a doctor. Your sponsor will be your guide through the step process. They may not even be complete on this, but I've found I turned to the Joe and Charlie App available on the App Store for a modest price, which helped complete answers to some of the questions my sponsor couldn't clarify. That being said, the depths I went to in my rock bottom before being introduced to AA played out exactly right for me to gain better reliance on a higher power. I've heard when the student is ready the teacher will appear, and vice versa.

Side note: this is a good time for honesty, open-mindedness, and willingness.

I've advised many clients to be observant and patient when looking for sponsorship. The things I think people should look for were things I once scoffed at. I'd sit smugly in the back of the meeting, looking at those up-front interacting and smiling and calling them the grinning idiots. I'd eventually have to give them credit for one thing: they looked happy, and they were not using a substance to achieve their happiness. I looked at some other things too. These men and women were gainfully employed, had good familial relations, solved problems with words, helped other people with no regard for gain, were not a burden on society at large, and behaved like ladies and gentlemen. This was not true of all people in the fellowship, but they did exist. When I polled them about how they became happy and admirable people, each one told me they all found a higher power and worked on the 12 Steps of recovery.

It wasn't long before I had the proof for giving the twelve steps a real try, and little did I know I completed Step 2 in doing so. I came to believe a power greater than myself could restore me to sanity. I by no means stumbled on knowledge of God, but I believed these people had something I did not and became willing to try what they tried. Looking back, I still didn't really believe it would work for me. At the very least, I wanted to be able to look my then-adult children in the eyes and tell them I did my level best to accomplish sobriety, happiness, and being a person they'd admire. I'd imagine it wouldn't ever work for me, and I'd just be telling them to move on and leave me to my bitter ends, but at least they'd know I tried.

While working on the steps, something happened, and I started to feel better. I remember somewhere between six and nine months, and I had begun making the amends steps eight and nine talk about, my wife looked at me and stated, "You are happy, aren't you?" I replied, "I think that's what this is." It had been so long since I had felt comfortable in my skin that I couldn't remember the feeling of true happiness. I had felt touches of this when my children were born, but these cases were so few and far between I couldn't remember them.

"No problem can be solved from the same level of consciousness that created it." ——*Albert Einstein*

The relationship between mentor and mentee will change as one advances through the steps and recovery as a whole. The dynamic between you and your sponsor will eventually outgrow being like a Jedi Master and apprentice. We certainly don't know as much about who taught Bruce Lee Kung fu or Bach's composition of music as we know about these two who are famed for what they did, yet they did have teachers. The teachers may not have reached their students' heights, but they were still humble enough to get them started down their paths of great success. The critical part of

Paul Moore

sponsorship was having someone who challenged my thinking and showed me how to try new things. The best way for me to be taught this was by example. A hypocrite might possess great knowledge of how to do something, but I cannot learn from a hypocrite because they don't practice what they preach. I needed people to demonstrate this way—the way they told me was a better way. I needed people to show me they could be happy without substances while also maintaining a job and a family. I didn't need perfection. I needed to see that I could progress.

Bill Wilson, the famed co-founder of Alcoholics Anonymous, was first sponsored by Ebby Thatcher. Ebby was a member of the Oxford Group, and many of the principles of the Alcoholics Anonymous program were derived from the practice of this group. Ebby never achieved lasting sobriety, but Bill took what he learned from him, added his own portions, and made something we see today that works for millions of former alcoholics. I say former alcoholics though most members of Alcoholics Anonymous still refer to themselves as Alcoholics even though they no longer abuse alcohol. Most say this keeps it fresh in their minds and keeps them from forgetting where they came from.

When Einstein said, "No problem can be solved from the same level of consciousness that created it," he was right. The knowledge I possessed, and the level of consciousness I attained were no longer enough to solve my problem with substances. I needed to level up, and that occurred by hanging out with others who had reached a new level of understanding themselves. "Birds of a feather flock together," is something my grandmother said to me. I've found this to be true. When we hang out with others, we either rise or sink to the level of the group. If I hang out with five millionaires, I'll probably be millionaire number six. Conversely, if I hang out with five drug addicts, I'm destined to leave or become addict number six.

There is safety in numbers so surround yourself with those who have what you aspire to yourself.

My mentorship throughout recovery wasn't solely dependent on my sponsor either. I got many numbers of those men and women who I saw behaving admirably. I've mentioned in the previous chapter the concept of not seeking sponsorship of anyone you may be sexually attracted to. In the case of my female mentors, I had circumstances where I wasn't sexually attracted to them, nor did we speak of things that would lead us to these conversations. As I said, they were admirable people and behaved "appropriately"—even when I didn't know what that meant. I also suffered from no sex drive during my first year sober and severe low self-esteem and anhedonia, which is a lack of pleasurable feelings, or really any feelings of any sort.

When my sponsor was busy, as he was a family man with four children, a wife, and a good career, I'd call other people on the same path for solutions. I didn't seek to be advised by those who would rubber-stamp my bullshit. In other words, I didn't ask guys who were cheating on their wives if it was good to go have an affair or guys who were still playing with some other substances whether I should do that too. I sought out those who would tell me the sometimes hard truths I needed to hear. Because the people I aligned with weren't afraid to tell me the truth, I heard the following phrase "Perhaps Paul, you should apologize for your behavior," quite often.

I do believe if you start the process of prayer even saying something as simple as "Please help me," you'll receive the guidance you need miraculously. The help that arrives probably won't feel or seem miraculous at all at first. Sometimes we are guided by those who need to teach us a lesson, and particularly in the beginning, these lessons are never much fun. I can see all my suffering even through post-acute withdrawal today in a positive light. This wasn't so while I was in the process of going through it. Time stretched immeasurably while I was in pain, but that happening allowed me a lot of gratitude for seemingly simple things when they returned. I became grateful to sit comfortably still in a chair. I became grateful to comprehend a paragraph I had just read. I became grateful to sleep more than fifteen minutes. This pain taught me a lesson in gratitude for what I had.

Having more than one trusted guide also helps those times your sponsor's advice is colored through their own problems and biases. A sponsor is just a human being and it's easy for us to put them on a pedestal, after all, they are helping us without charge or material gain. That being said, they are not always right about everything. Even during the times my sponsor has been wrong, I respect the man enough to just seek the solution elsewhere. As I've written about earlier, you'll not always be Jedi and Padawan apprentice with your sponsor. My sponsor now shares his problems with me. Oftentimes he just has to hear his own advice given back to him in my voice. I've learned other things in seeking spiritual guidance and read a great many books on the subject and sometimes I have something new to add. But it was still his initial guidance that allowed me to seek that knowledge and therefore I pay him the respect I believe he's entitled to.

The fact that my sponsor doesn't need his name mentioned in this book is very telling about his character. While he's not perfect, he was perfect for my spiritual development. He's led me through this process in such a way that resembles Plutarch's quote, "The mind is not a vessel to be filled, but a fire to be ignited." I've heard others describe recovery in different sayings. You've probably heard them too: "It's like walking up the down escalator." "Stop practicing and you go back to where you started." "I don't stay sober on yesterday's recovery." "I don't stay clean on yesterday's shower." "I don't stay fit from yesterday's workout." There are many ways to address recovery and it is indeed something you have to do for yourself, but there is help and guidance. I never forget where I was and came from and I do my best never to put myself on a pedestal. I believe if I stop doing what has sustained me in my recovery, I'll revisit places I don't want to go.

What are some of the qualities you value in this mentorship? Take some time to write them down.

_____

_____

_____

_____

_____

_____

_____

_____

_____

_____

_____

_____

_____

_____

_____

_____

_____

_____

_____

_____

_____

_____

"One of the hardest things was learning that I was worth recovery."

— Demi Lovato

CHAPTER SEVEN

Personal Responsibility

Early in my recovery, I was shown a comprehensive list of everything I was entitled to. It was a blank sheet of paper with no mention of happiness, naked ladies feeding me grapes, a boatload of cash, or a suitcase full of cocaine! I didn't like this very much at all. I blamed circumstances and people for my problems for most of my life but did very little myself to change them. I was told, however, I could fill up the page with anything I was willing to work for. As I've said before, recovery is a daily process. We don't stay clean on yesterday's shower. I wish I could pay someone to work out for me or eat right for me, but science hasn't presented a way for this to occur. I had to start doing better a little at a time. This didn't mean I took it all on at once. I took baby steps and did what I was able to do each day. Baby steps included going to meetings, starting to pray, and working on things for as long as I could by breaking them into manageable increments.

I learned more about my higher power through these baby steps. I figured if He made me able-bodied and able to get something done myself, I was blessed. I needed to stop complaining about my childhood, my other illnesses, the opportunities lost due to my addiction, and poor treatment from employers, police, and everyone else. I had to really learn to accept accountability for my wellness. I thought self-reliance sounded contrary to reliance on a higher power, but I learned it is not. My higher power still put people, opportunities for growth, and healing in my path. There is a paradox to love. I learned along the way that the more I give, the more I have to give to others—including myself.

I was still responsible for doing what was necessary to facilitate my growth and thinking. There were many seemingly magical occurrences that happened for me along the way, and I'll write more on those in the upcoming chapters. Suffice it to say that if I did what was necessary, a power greater than myself would do what was necessary to aid in my recovery. During my time in the fellowship, I've heard many others saying things that go along with this idea too. God will guide the boat, but he doesn't do the rowing, and why should He when he's given me two good arms and a strong back to do the work.

I learned the hard way I was a very arrogant, entitled individual. I went through several stays in treatment, blaming the counselors and staff's poor performance when I failed repeatedly. Like working out, the staff couldn't recover for me. I needed to make a commitment to myself. How much we love someone usually determines the level of inconvenience we will go through for them. I'll certainly go through a lot of inconvenience for my wife or my children, but it wasn't until I inconvenienced myself for myself, I started to get better. I needed to admit truths that were hard to admit. I wondered, "Do I even really know what love is if I don't love myself?"

Talk about an inconvenience, tonight I'm writing this from an emergency room in the hospital. I have been extremely stressed about the work I do. The level of stress I'm under makes me seek proper guidance, and mental help might make others laugh. I love myself enough at this point in my life and career to not risk what I worked so hard to attain. I've learned to ask when I need a hand to get through life. Receiving support isn't shirking my responsibilities. It is merely taking a break and seeking guidance when necessary.

I haven't found many people with good, comfortable, sustained sobriety who haven't accepted personal responsibility for it. While many things are seemingly outside our control, especially when looking at injury during childhood and other traumas of that sort. While things done to me while I was young and helpless were outside my ability to control or impact, carrying them through into adulthood and living as a victim, seeking pity,

Paul Moore

was definitely not beyond my control. I only had myself to blame for continuing this behavior.

I'd often use my mental illness as a crutch. I interrupt people talking because of my lack of impulse control from my ADHD. Was this true? More than likely, yes, it was true. Did this make those I interrupted all the time want to converse with me? No! Is there anything I can do to help curb this behavior? Maybe learn to listen to someone else unselfishly. Talk to people newer in the fellowship than myself, and they are usually still selfish enough to make the entire conversation about themselves. I could practice doing better. What a novel idea. I've since even realized for my YouTube recovery show, I could grab a chess timer to ensure the other guest as much speaking time as I'd use myself.

Everything I blamed on addiction and mental illness, I could practice doing better. Even my chemical imbalances could be regulated through diet, exercise, and routine. While I couldn't totally control the endorphins in my head by thought, I could do specific actions to release more. I could do some pushups every morning, make my bed, and show up regardless of how I felt when I committed to being somewhere. I knew one thing for sure: even if I wanted to stay in bed all day, going where I committed to, would, at the very least, make sure I didn't feel worse. Every time I did this, I'd feel a bit better as well. While the circus is still in town, as many still call me crazy, it's a lot friendlier than it once was. It's downright manageable.

As I sit here in the hospital's emergency department, I'm watching two current alcoholics share their tales of woe with everyone who will listen. I hope maybe a light gets turned on for them as they receive treatment. I watch everyone else roll their eyes and shake their head at their behavior, and I remember when I was still like this. I have to realize the limited potential for being a vehicle for change for those who are not ready for it.

Be kind to yourself

I hope by now you've tried a little meditation. I'll expand further on this in an upcoming chapter, but for now, write down five things that make you happy. Not five things that "should" make you happy, but five things that actually bring a smile to your face. It could be your car, your phone, your child, a guitar, a color you like, whatever feels good—the sky is the limit. Now close your eyes, breathe deeply into your stomach, and try to take longer to breathe out than breathing in. You are meditating!

What are those five or ten things that make you happy?

_____

_____

_____

_____

_____

_____

_____

Even breathing deeply and writing what makes you happy for two minutes a day will help you with what I'd like you to start doing for yourself. I'll write more about the benefits of this daily practice in your life later. Now, back to being kind to yourself. If you have a friend who is self-conscious and a few pounds overweight, I'm certain you don't say to them, "Wow, you're fat and look terrible. Why are you eating so much junk food?" Yet when I looked in the mirror at myself, I'd say these horrible things to myself. Disparaging myself or others disparaging me had little to no effect on curbing my addiction. But love—love would cut through the deepest chemical fog I'd ever been intoxicated with.

It was always those few poignant moments of loving kindness in my active addiction that would get me through the booze, the coke, the heroin, and all of it. One night I'll never forget my adult daughter caught me intoxicated, bringing liquor into the house. She broke down, which she didn't often do in front of me as I had compromised her emotional security in my using and drinking. This time though, she cried and asked me, "Why are we not enough? Why do you need this? We love you." I'll never forget those words or the lack of a good response to give her as the reason I continued to use substances to escape and unknowingly caused my family to feel the way my daughter expressed to me. I know now the reason was I didn't love myself, nor did I think taking myself away from my family was actually taking something tangible away from them. Over time and being kind to myself, I learned differently.

Expressing kindness toward myself started simply by being mindful of what words I was using on myself that I'd never use on someone I considered a friend. Men jest pretty hard with each other, but if I know something really bothers someone, the matter stays out of my joking. I learned this slowly over time. I remember being in a partial hospital setting, a day camp for the mentally ill. I was at one of the lowest points in my life. I was very suicidal and was starting to convince myself that the world, my family, and everyone else would be better off without dealing with me. Thus, I was convincing myself—knowing the ramifications suicide leaves as a legacy on those left behind.

This clinician, I can't even remember or picture their face in my mind, asked me to write a letter to a friend who was feeling exactly like I was. My letter said things like, "Just hang on. We need you; we love you, try again, don't give up, etcetera." As I read my letter, I wondered, "Why wasn't I telling myself those same things?"

I had to start paying attention to how I'd speak to myself. At first, I'd constantly slip into self-deprecating and disparaging speech. It started slowly, but I stopped saying horrible things to myself. If I was trying to lose some weight, I'd tell myself, "Boy, you are looking slim!" when I'd catch my appearance in the mirror. The fact that it wasn't true just made me laugh, which was a great side effect.

Through this practice, you will start to love yourself, and from that self-love, your love for others will bloom and grow. However, if the behavior is out of line with your spirit, this will not work. If you've defrauded someone out of money or cheated on someone you love, you simply won't be able to say, "Oh well, I'm a nice guy," and believe it. This practice does, however, help with self-forgiveness when we realize an act was wrong. We can take that to meditation and speak to ourselves saying things like, "I don't like that behavior in myself." "I'm going to try not to do it again."

and, "I'll apologize if it doesn't hurt the other person." Telling your girlfriend you cheated just to ease your own conscience when she doesn't know is just selfishness. There are other ways to amend for behavior we haven't been caught doing.

"When you recover or discover something that nourishes your soul and brings joy, care enough about yourself to make room for it in your life."

— Jean Shinoda Bolen

CHAPTER EIGHT

What makes you happy?

One of the best things to ever happen to me was something that felt like, at the time, one of the worst things to happen to me. In my first year sober, my only friend was Sir Chremesickle. He was my big orange cat, and he pretty much loved me unconditionally. I say pretty much because he'd spitefully pee on my stuff when I left him for a day or two and was standoffish when I arrived home. He'd warm up soon enough and be back to being my buddy. He'd let me squeeze him and give him hugs, and he'd spoon with me and put his paw in my hand. He'd follow me to bed and stop to wait for me. He also liked and recognized Ben and Jerry's strawberry cheesecake ice cream, and he knew he was getting the lid when I opened a fresh pint. Sir Chremesickle was one of those faces of God I got to see. Thank God, he loved me as nobody else liked me very much at all.

While my wife was still willing to put a roof over my head in early recovery, she told me point blank there was no way possible to reconcile our relationship. My children were counseling her to divorce me. Needless to say, they didn't like me much either. At the time, the feeling was pretty mutual. I felt they were forcing me to get sober, and I wasn't very fond of them either. While they had put up with me, in the end, love meant food and shelter and little else. Knowing I couldn't fix things with some grand gesture, I set out to find out what made me happy.

It had been so long since I'd been sober that I had no idea what made me happy. When I was high on cocaine, cleaning my house made me happy, this wasn't true when not high on cocaine. My early days in recovery were a time to discover who I was. While this was uncomfortable, I value this time greatly and will always be grateful to my wife for giving me this gift to discover myself. Four years into the program and it turns out she is still my wife, and I'm grateful for that.

Knowing I couldn't earn anyone's love back through some grand, but self-serving gesture, as most all my gestures were self-serving at the time, I knew I had to please myself. I wasn't sure what I even liked. I really couldn't remember. I didn't even really like some of what I liked but did for accolades or prestige. I kind of like making art and playing music, but I don't like it enough to sit around and do it just for the joy of creation. I liked the accolades, the "oohs" and "ahs" I'd receive when people saw me make it. There will be no doubt when you find your calling because you'll have to do it no matter what. Without the barest shadow of a doubt, I now know what I love to do.

I love to serve and heal others.

Whether this form of serving or healing is writing, speaking, creating solutions toward wellness, or giving someone a ride to detox, this is what I must do. Serving in these ways is where my knowledge and value lie. The time has passed on me being the best father I can be. I have repaired and will continue to practice that to the best of my ability. As a husband, I improve as I go along and will continue to do so. My relationship is very important, though not as important as my relationship with myself and with God. If I don't help myself, I'm of little use to those around me, and I'm also probably miserable to be around.

I figured this out slowly as events came to pass in my life. I enjoyed going to 12-step meetings, and I was led to believe I had value in this fellowship. I was told even the smallest things I did were of value, like showing up and being present to listen, respecting those who shared their experiences, picking up chairs and putting out the garbage, and giving someone a ride to a meeting. These small acts were all valuable, and I found I was valued for participating. I also had no baggage with those ladies and gentlemen at meetings. I hadn't deprived them of emotional security as I had my own family. I hadn't vomited on their carpets or stolen money from them. I was treated for the most part based on how I'd act from the day I arrived instead of based on my past addictive behaviors. When I behaved like a gentleman, I was usually treated like a gentleman. This also made it a refuge away from much of the damage I'd caused in my home. I needed this refuge where I could feel good about myself and my behavior.

Next, I started volunteering at a local food pantry run by my uncle at my former church. My goal wasn't pure altruism. I was bored, looking for things to do, and had the ulterior motive of wanting to heal a once damaged relationship. That relationship didn't get very much healing in the year or so I went every Tuesday.

What did happen was I enjoyed the people who would come in for commodities each week. For the most part, the patrons were senior citizens who came for a little extra help. They'd get very little, but they were usually extremely grateful for what they got. A jar of peanut butter, a can of tuna, some pasta, and just a few staples to help their ends meet on a fixed income. I was pretty cheerful when I did this, I loved the woman I handed out food with, and she loved me back.

Her name was Sandy, and sometimes the things I told her about my addiction were shocking to her, but I was always truthful. She and her husband picked me up one Christmas Eve and took me to the service. The Christmas music, the candlelight, and the spirit of the people brought the service to life. Christmas Eve service was one I always loved because I easily felt the presence of God while I was there.

This service I did at the church every Tuesday also made me feel loved and valued. I never did restore my relationship with my uncle to the one I envisioned we had when I was a child. Still, it awakened me with what we had and how much he actually valued me. I was starting to value myself, and through valuing myself, I started valuing others the same way. I started to realize I was actually a pretty smart person, and I should be treated how my behavior dictated. Volunteering also set me up on a pretty healthy routine which helped combat my depression. I was starting to honor my word and the commitments I made. So, even if I felt a bit depressed those Tuesday mornings, I still rolled out of bed and handed out food, even if I didn't take a shower some mornings because I was dragging ass.

Doing what I committed to made me feel better about myself. This follow-through and commitment to myself lifted my esteem enough to be ready for the next opportunity when it presented itself. The next opportunity was to get training for a peer recovery certification. This was a free class offered by a non-profit group called Parents Support Network, which provided many people of low-income extra help with their skills as parents. They also trained those to coach other addicts and alcoholics into recovery, as many of the parents were dealing with child services to get their kids back.

During the six weeks of classes, I made many good friends during training and loved providing them with delicious home-baked treats. I still needed to get 500 hours working in the field before I could test for my certification. I did this all a little at a time. Problems arose, but solutions presented themselves too. I was getting some momentum now. The momentum came from seeing that I could accomplish some things I set my mind to. This momentum came a little at a time, and while it was hard to break the inertia of depression and being at a standstill, it could occur even if the start was very small.

Through adversity, my experience with trauma and different facets of addiction uniquely prepared me to apply for a paid internship with Parents Support Network. I was well-versed in addiction, trauma, sexual confusion, homelessness, imprisonment, body dysmorphia, mental illness, and more. Though more than 500 applied for the internship, it was awarded to me on the spot during the interview. While the money was nothing to write home about, I was getting paid to use my experience and help others.

I arrived home, fell on my knees, and thanked a God I didn't believe in because everything I once blamed him for was now going to be useful. The internship fell through because of Covid restrictions, but that wasn't enough to stop me. At this point, I had momentum. I simply found another job where I could get my hours, take my test, and make it happen. I cried tears of joy, stunned at how my pain was made useful. The pain of everyone's ire with me also set me to love myself. Today I understand what they mean when they say, "How can you love when you don't love yourself?"

Once this level of insight starts occurring, there is no stopping you. I've learned kindness from the cruel. Tolerance from the intolerant. Love from the hateful. Today my greatest teachers are usually jerks who can rile me up. When we don't get easily riled up any longer, those we call jerks become our greatest teachers.

Now, I only really look inward when something is out of kilter, when life is smooth, I needn't stop for self-examination.

"Embrace YOU...Believe in yourself, in this very moment...forgive yourself for all mistakes and 'bad' decisions you may have made in the past. Do not allow others opinions or judgements of who you were yesterday or decades ago define who you are today. Each and every day opens new doors for miracles of healing to occur in our lives. Embrace these miracles, big or small, even those you may presently be unaware of. Live in this moment, for this is all we have. Give thanks to your Higher Power for all that you are, for the very breath that allows life, love, and abundance to flow to you and through you forever more.
Live in the Light of All That IS."

—Angie Karan

CHAPTER NINE

A Higher Power That Works

I came upon this very individual process after shirking my former religious associations. I was raised Lutheran and watched Christians behave horribly, hypocritically, cruelly, fearfully, wrathfully, lusty, bigoted, and every other deadly sin. To top it off, I didn't really understand past my judgment of these flawed individuals, especially being one myself. I thought if there was a God, he was some mean kid on his throne trying to spoil my fun with a bunch of seemingly arbitrary rules. I have since come to an understanding that God is within each and every one of us. Because I have a spark of divinity in me, I'll not be very happy if I violate certain rules he laid out. I have a good tell for that, though. If something makes my gut hurt, I probably shouldn't do it.

Psychiatric professionals will call this gut feeling many things like conscience, values, and intuition, and believe it's the set of values instilled during childhood. I've come to think it's more the spark of divinity. If you think you have no contact with this source, I'll bet you are wrong. How much guilt, shame, and remorse did you feel when you acted out of line with your values? To me, these negative feelings are God telling me firsthand, "Don't do that." I was always mystified when people behaved admirably. They didn't imbibe strong substances. They didn't cheat on their girlfriends, and they were honest in their business interactions. These things were immeasurably hard for me. I wondered, "How'd they do that?" It turns out they followed their conscience and practiced behaving according to it.

Last night I sat in the emergency room waiting room for an inordinate amount of time—all said, it was fifteen hours of mostly waiting. I was pretty content, though. I brought a couple of books to read as well as electronic devices. I wrote a chapter of this book, I read about 200 pages of Tolstoy, and I meditated for several hours I was there. I had the equanimity to not complain and to actually apologize to the understaffed hospital workers for burdening them with my trivial problem. I don't go to doctors regularly, and I needed a referral I couldn't wait for. While I was there, an alcoholic significantly under the influence came into the ER escorted by security. He was a marine veteran of Afghanistan. He was absolutely belligerent, calling the female staff names, and making the security staff very angry. They met this defiance with defiance; never a good plan with someone who is in that state; without certain attributes, it's usually best to let them sleep it off.

During this time, I was still meditating while watching what was transpiring. When it looked like all was about to go sideways and erupt in violence, I asked the security staff if I could have a word with him. I was in scrubs with a badge on, dressed for work, and they consented as they were having little luck getting him to sit quietly and await treatment. Though enraged, he was seated and too inebriated to stand. I could feel the rage, which really was pain, emanating from him. Each time he brought up fighting for this country and watching his friends die, I felt it stab me in the stomach. I pulled a table up to him, sat very close to him, and I spoke very softly. I didn't know where these words were coming from, but they were the right words. I thanked him for his service and asked his name. He told me it was Ricky. I looked long into his eyes, and I told him, "I know what you are going through with the drinking." I told him he was worthwhile, and we just wanted to help him. I put my hand on his arm, and when our faces were about a foot apart, I said, "It's going to be okay."

Upon hearing my reassurances, he broke down and fell into my arms. This grizzled tough marine war veteran let me hold him, and we cried together. Looking into his eyes, I was able to see a facet of the almighty, and I was able to give him mercy and love while his behavior showed he deserved neither. His rage went out of him like a candle in the wind. I purchased him a drink and candy bar from the vending machine, and he simply passed out, exhausted from the anger.

Ricky got thrown out several hours later after the hospital staff had enough. I pray he is okay and gets the help he needs one day. I did what I could to serve, and something contrary to my human nature was able to provide the loveless with love. Looking at the course of my life, it's easy to know and feel this was something more powerful than me. This was pure love without seeking recognition, acting only to serve. Serving in this way with no ulterior motive is what I've been called to do. As a bonus, serving him was a great natural high for me.

I think the bottom line is on every chip they hand out at Alcoholics Anonymous meetings. It's a line from Shakespeare's Hamlet, "To thine own self be true." Reading a great many spiritual books helped me separate man and religion from the doctrines these great teachers taught. More importantly, the things they said to practice worked. I got empirical proof the noble eightfold path made me feel better and that Christ's teaching of loving your enemy made me feel better. I also found I could only really connect to this source if I practiced certain principles. I had to adjust my behavior in line with that spark of the divine that is in each of us. No, I don't believe people are born sociopathic. I believe they have dulled out the conscious contact with a higher source and hardened themselves against it.

While I'm still a bit out of sorts with some things happening in my life, it turns out the discord is mostly about my ego. Ego in Alcoholics Anonymous meetings I've attended has become the acronym Edge God Out. I've found this to be true for most other people and me. If something is about my recognition, my accolades, my material gains, actually almost anything where I'm saying "I," "Me," or "Mine," it's going to cause discord. As hard as it is to practice forgiveness, understanding, love, and selfless behavior, it makes me happier to do it than when I get wrapped up in my own self-pity.

Being connected is being in love, and if I'm headed toward a relapse, I'm probably sitting isolated in self-pity, telling everyone my tale of woe. Bill Wilson found the cure for this one night while he was away on business, and the bar was beckoning to him. He made a phone call and asked if there were any alcoholics that he could go talk to. It turns out there was, and he became the co-founder of Alcoholics Anonymous, Doctor Bob Smith.

Sometimes those we are trying to help will relapse, die, and go through years of more turmoil, but if it keeps me sober to try to help others. It also makes me happier and stops me from being restless, irritable, or discontent, and it has saved my life for another day.

Why not pray, why not meditate, why not feel good. This is the connection that can help save your life for another day.

"Blame equals pain. Lies equal pain. Secrets equal pain. It's as simple as that."

—Brianne Davis

CHAPTER TEN

Honesty, Open-mindedness, and Willingness

(Steps one, two, and three)

As Alcoholics Anonymous says in how it works, by using honesty, open-mindedness, and willingness, you are well on your way. These attributes apply to all the steps, but especially to the first three. Deciding to embark on this lifestyle change requires all three for recovery. It can be hard to undertake this journey if you are on the fence about whether your life needs some change. This is why it's imperative to be as honest as you can with yourself about what you need to recover from. The substances are out of your system within a few days of detox. For some of us who used these substances addictively, our brains will also have some healing. Fortunately, the latest science says our brains are very malleable and have great healing capacity. There is also no need to be a genius to accomplish this goal. I know many people of average intelligence who have had no problems undertaking this work. It's more about good guidance and a little bit of practice.

Step 1: We admitted we were powerless over alcohol, and that our lives have become unmanageable."

I didn't have much trouble accepting I was addicted to drugs and alcohol by the time I came into the fellowship. What was harder to admit was whether or not my life was unmanageable because of them. I fought against this notion for years, mainly because I was so afraid of life without my crutch. To be perfectly honest, I undertook the steps only because I was at my wit's end, and my choices became so limited. I knew once I took the first drink or drug, I didn't know what would happen. Not knowing what will happen after putting a substance in my system is a good definition of addiction is, in my opinion, a very good description of uncontrolled addiction. Sometimes nothing would happen. I'd simply veg out on the easy chair, enjoy my oblivion, and eventually fall asleep without issue. But in the end, more often than not, there were more dire consequences—driving under the influence and the accompanying legal charges, failed relationships, failures in my career, and failed friendships where people couldn't accept my drug and alcohol use and abuse. Embarrassment came often. I was expelled from my home, and my wife planned on divorce. My children didn't like me or want to spend time with me. These were some things that made me consider the unmanageability of substance use.

I also had to look at the unmanageability of being sober. I experienced this in my twenties when I had seven unmanageable years of white-knuckle sobriety. I was still in conflict with most nouns in general, considering nouns represent people, places, things, and ideas. I still had poor communication, was angry much of the time, and my outlook on life was filled with gloom and doom. I was still seeking approval and being disingenuous with others about my feelings and what I wanted in life. The truth was I had very little clue what I wanted. I knew what I didn't want, and that was the misery I was feeling on a day-to-day basis. I wrongly was under the impression that if my circumstances changed, I'd be happy. Conditions were changing, though. I met my lovely wife, sought a degree, got it, went to the gym, got in great shape, held a decent job, and more. Still, I wasn't content or at peace. When I finally was offered some opiates at my doctor's, I practically jumped for them. My life was unmanageable with or without substances to a greater and lesser degree. I was the only constant in my life. Alcohol is only mentioned in the first step; the rest of the steps relate to how we deal with people, places, ideas, and institutions. I didn't even really meet the most basic requirement for membership which was a desire to stop drinking. I did desire it more than I desired to beg for money on the street corner. Blessedly it turned out that was enough.

I'll need to be honest about my level of honesty. The fact for me was it seemed to come in levels. The first level was integral that my life was unmanageable with drugs and alcohol, and I didn't do such a great job at it even free of these substances. That's a pretty bitter pill to swallow. All I knew about living life was going to have to be put under the microscope and evaluated. It's a good thing I could revisit my life piecemeal. I did a little at a time. I didn't overwhelm myself trying to do it all at once. "Easy does it, but do it," comes to mind. These little cliches became pretty deep in meaning as I think back on the process. Cliches become cliches because there is truth in them. If they were not true, they wouldn't continuously be used to become cliches.

I wasn't "cash register honest" when I walked into my first meeting. All putting down the substances did was make me a more cognizant liar, cheat, and thief. Now my brain was less cloudy, and I could be better at all these negative behaviors. Shaping my virtues came later as I got more honest and had to admit some of these behaviors were not making me happy, joyous, and free. These basic admissions were required to embark on the journey. I had enough ground to have Step 1 and move on to the second step, where open-mindedness became necessary.

Step 2: "Came to believe a power greater than ourselves could restore us to sanity."

Even considering Step 2 took an open mind for sure. I had been brought up Lutheran and had gone to Sunday school and confirmation, mostly because I was made to go. During this training, I came to believe if God existed, he certainly was a big downer. I imagined God a lot like Santa, taking notes on all the times I masturbated, did someone wrong, lusted over those I wanted to have sex with etcetera, etcetera. I hadn't gotten anywhere with praying, as I had prayed all the time, first a rote prayer nightly, then anytime I was in trouble. It never seemed to do any good at all. By the time I was an adolescent, I had found out I could do what I wanted and then, at the end of my life, say I was sorry and be forgiven. This is what I set out to do. Living the way I chose to live would make me sorry. Eventually, I learned that I was supposed to live a decent life because I have a soul, and acting against that spark of divinity within would be to my detriment. I wasn't getting away with anything living this way.

The next part of this required some honest observation. When I went to the meetings, I observed people who could do things I could not do well free of a substance in me. These folks were laughing, smiling, comfortable in their skin, at peace, solving problems with words, gainfully employed, had good family relationships, and were not a burden on society. Upon this observation, I had to ask what they were doing and how they were doing it. Every single one, they all prayed and worked on themselves using the steps. Their answers gave me what I needed to believe Step 2 was true, at least for these people. That's all it took to open the door to hope. If they could do this, maybe I could too, and maybe I'd get a little bit of what they had. I started praying every day, certain it wouldn't work for me. I was now becoming willing.

Step 3: Made a decision to turn our will and our lives over to the care of

God, as we understood him.

Sometimes people think this means I suddenly gave my will over to God. Nope, I made a decision is what I did. I didn't know the will of God from the will of anyone else. Sure, I'd read some great moral tales in the Bible, usually about guys who seemed way better at doing these things than I would ever be. If they had a sliding scale and held me up to Noah, Jesus, Buddha, or any of these teachers, I failed miserably. I liked to get high, I liked the enjoyment I got from casual sex, I was greedy, I wasn't very charitable, and I might have well been the opposite of any of these examples from the Bible. That was okay because I didn't have a flash of light and suddenly was living a virtuous life. I had only made the decision to do so. Actually, doing it involved a lot of practice and many failures.

I was a very good shoplifter while I was using drugs. I had my own little method of never getting caught that seemed to work very well. I'd put the things I didn't want to pay for under the heavy bag of dog food or cat food. If the checkout clerk looked, I'd pay for it. If they didn't, I would not. I didn't have much fear about doing this, and I had justified that I was getting screwed paying the store's high prices.

After getting sober, my daughter, who knew of my shoplifting skill, took me with her to the store. She said if you steal anything, even if you don't get caught, I'll never take you to the store again. At this point, I had to make a decision between saving $12 on walnuts vs. having a relationship with my daughter. Our relationship wasn't great at this point anyway, but I was hopeful it could improve. I refrained from shoplifting on our trip to the store. This was the practical side of doing God's will. It was written in the Ten Commandments, and most people just don't do it, either from fear or good common sense. I didn't have much of these things, so I needed to learn how to behave properly from others who did.

I was ready to embark now on the dreaded fourth step, and take an inventory of all my shortcomings. I'd start getting to know God's will as I went along through proper mentorship, modeling, and good old-fashioned failing. While this held a lot of fear for me, I discovered that doing a little work was better than thinking about doing the work. I did, after all, have quite a vivid imagination and was prone to fatalistic thinking.

"Realize that you are only resentful to the extent you've given your power away. If you're in full possession of your personal power, you can afford to be generous when someone else is behaving poorly. It's only when you're not owning your power fully that it shows up as resentment."

— Katherine Woodward Thomas

CHAPTER ELEVEN

Housecleaning

Throughout my recovery, I've spent some time reviewing the fourth step; I've studied the method brought to light by the big book, expounded on *The Twelve Steps and Twelve Traditions*, and looked at Russell Brand's book, *Recovery: Freedom from Our Addictions*, and listened to Joe and Charlie, many, many times. Even when looking at the purest form of this step and speaking with many who have taken it as such, I've found many differences in how exactly they did their fourth steps. That being said, I think the fourth step, "Made a searching and fearless moral inventory of ourselves," is about developing new insights that allow a happy existence.

I think it's integral that this step is taken with someone who has successfully completed it themselves. Here's what it looks like to have successfully completed this step. This individual can be judged as reasonable. They have equanimity, which is peace of mind—even in chaos. They usually live a healthy life, improve familial relations, are gainfully employed, not a burden on society, and continue to help others. These attributes were what was once judged as recovered from a seemingly hopeless state of mind and body. Today, many in the fellowship look first at years sober to measure success. During my time, I've found many who have many years of abstinence from substances but very little peace of mind. I wouldn't turn to these people to find the difference I sought because they frankly didn't have it.

In reading quite a lot on self-help, psychology, and spirituality, it has been said you cannot have two conflicting thoughts simultaneously. While you are angry and hateful, you won't feel love and gratitude. While cruel, you won't feel kindness, etcetera. This process of Step 4 frees oneself of the near-constant anger and resentment addicts dwell in, often without realizing it. It's usually only upon a written review of these resentments are burning us up that we realize we have quite a few.

Not only do we have resentments, we hold onto them in unhealthy ways and perpetuate the negative patterns. For example, perhaps I want to hold onto the anger of sexual abuse because it provides the rationale for my conduct. I might think to myself, "Well, I'm promiscuous because this happened," or "I drink because this happened." I'm not trying to discount the pain that one went through because of painful events that occurred throughout our lives. I'm saying we must accept and even forgive these events so we do not use them as a reason to continue harming ourselves. If we want contented sobriety, we must look at these issues and the ways we've used them to rationalize and justify our often poor conduct.

When recovery became more important than resentment, I needed to ask, "Do I want to be angry, or at peace?" Indeed, I sometimes loved my anger—especially while I dwelled in it. It felt powerful to be angry. Especially when others frequently cowered from it. Anger provided me excuses to continue abusing substances or continue with other behaviors that led me back to self-destruction. I'll tell you, this process of doing the work in Step 4 made me comfortable in my skin and helped me begin replacing fear with courage and faith. Had I taken this integral step many years ago, many things could have been different when I first entered the fellowship, and I could have avoided years of pain and turmoil. Though I didn't, I still live today free of regret due in large part to fully integrating these steps in my life.

It would have been nice to have been the father I could have been to my children. I could and should have been their greatest cheerleader and encourager. Though I was not, I am that today, and though I'm not perfect, I have a method to change when I see I am wrong. The father I am to them today is beneficial. I'm a father who realizes when I've been wrong, where and how I've been wrong and changes that behavior. Somehow much of the turmoil they went through, as did I, affected all of us toward good ends.

Is this odd, or is this God? Today I believe benevolence and weaving of events that work everything out for the greatest good of everyone involved is a source of love that pervades our universe.

My daughter had adult burdens laid on her at a tender age. She dealt with my addiction and my depression. These burdens should have never been put upon her. Today, she is supremely independent due to many of these troubles; she is self-assured and confident because she has seen what she is capable of, despite a lack of support from me. These travails she experienced affected her negatively and positively. While she's still dealing with much of the wreckage from my less than stellar parenting, I am now available to help and show her the errors of my ways.

I will repeat myself greatly in this chapter, imploring you to do this work with another who is qualified. I've recommended many resources and taken many apart for you. Step 4 should be done with the support of a good mentor (sponsor)! The guidance and format I'm providing are meant to be aids and not a replacement for good guidance. In writing this chapter, I've seen how I didn't do this step perfectly when I did it. I, however, did it perfectly enough to enjoy the peace and promises that came from it. I replaced scorn and anger with love and gratitude. I replaced fear with faith and courage—which has made a huge difference in my recovery.

The dreaded inventory of our shortcomings, character defects, sins, moral failings, or any other term applied can be daunting to approach. I've found that the fear of putting pen to paper is worse than actually putting pen to paper. My former doom and gloom perspective would make a mountain of evil out of any molehill I considered. The anxiety I'd feel thinking about how bad it would be was always worse than the experience itself. I considered incomplete and imperfect work a sin, which created avoidance and procrastination on my part. If we truly even look at the origin of the word sin, it's an old English archery term for "off the mark, not dead center." I've found the idea of shooting the shot imperfectly and continuing to improve can be helpful.

There are many great resources for help in this step. It can be a bit confusing trying to do this yourself from the big book of Alcoholics Anonymous. The Joe and Charlie app is available for download on your device, which will take you through an in-depth look at all of the steps. There are many guides and worksheets available on the web as well. As usual, I recommend a good sponsor or mentor who has been through this process to help guide you. You can consider me one, and I'll put some journal prompts to help you along the way.

Just so you know, a sponsor may not be perfect at doing this either. There may be areas they haven't looked at themselves, and they cannot teach what they don't know. Looking for added resources can't hurt. I cannot say I did this step perfectly when I went through them myself. I did the best I knew how at the time. Occasionally when a big problem would arise, I'd break out the pen and paper again and write through this integral step again. As I continued to practice this process in my life, it got better.

Before digging in, I will give you the most simple and thorough overview I can of the fourth step. I have pieced this together from my own experience. This chapter is the most researched because I think a thorough appraisal of yourself is what brings you the ultimate freedom from substances.

When you went to meetings and started to listen to the stories others with addiction shared and related to the emotions they felt which drove them to change their lives, you may have, as I did, started to find a place where you belonged. Others had embarrassed themselves as I did. Others had bad relationships, as I had. Others had run-ins with the law, as I had. Others felt lonely, even in a crowd, and others experienced depression and anxiety. Others felt despair like I had. Suddenly, I didn't feel so alone or like the only person who'd fucked up their life. Hearing others felt as I once did but had a complete and psychic change of perspective made me more willing to work on myself.

That being said, I still had a few deep dark corners of behavior and thoughts I hadn't shared or heard shared, where I still felt separate from others. These were deep dark secrets I was going to take to the grave. Through the process with Step 4, I began to look at these secrets. Later, in Step 5, I shared them with another human being, and I really felt like I fit in. I finally became equal to everyone else on planet earth. Through Step 4, I became an integral part of, not separate from, the human race. I was no worse than the President or CEO. At the same time, I was no better than the vagrant on the street.

Through my work in Step 4, I also got to see how my selfish behavior hurt others pretty terribly. As I became as good as anyone else residing on planet earth, I realized just how much I deprived those I cared for and what I deprived them of. The biggest thing I denied them of was me, but when you don't value yourself, that never comes into consideration.

Many of the notions that drove me to drink or to use and abuse substances have gone away. I was driven to use drugs and to drink because of feelings I wanted to make go away. The addictions made the feelings disappear— at least temporarily. I would feel comfortably numbed out and rich in a synthetic bath of endorphin to alleviate those feelings through substance use. Of course, this was toxic and harmful to me, my relationships, my security, my reputation, and my ambitions. Many of these fears I took on from living my life turned out to be erroneous. I feared I needed another so I wouldn't be lonely and die alone. I feared I was flawed and, therefore, unlovable. The feeling I wasn't capable of taking care of myself and accomplishing dreams was untrue or only partially true.

Working my way through this brought some of these unconscious fears to the light of day, where they could be rationally evaluated and dispelled. I set out to make a list of what offended me, what really got my goat, and what I resented. Resentments are akin to anger and hatred, and the glaring ones come up again and again. At the very least, these items on my list are a giant waste of time. That's time that could be spent happy, dreaming, endeavoring toward goals, loving, and helping others was spent angrily recalling situations where I felt I was injured unjustly. When these fester in my mind, they are subject to my delusional thinking as time passes.

When you hear another talk of something they resent, it's sometimes easier to see this delusion at work. A relative of mine, who has a somewhat acerbic personality, came to me about a problem they were angry about.

This person usually makes their own mess of things and is often selfish and self-centered. By the time they spoke to me about this great upset, they had made themselves the innocent victim of a horrible incident.

The incident was this. They went to a donut shop and needed to use the restroom. There was no customer restroom at this shop, so they were denied use of a restroom. Therefore they went outside, climbed a wall for privacy, micturated into a cup, and proceeded to bring their urine back inside the donut shop and criticize the employee for making them pee into the receptacle.

They fully expected me to be on their side when they explained this to me. They had deluded themselves into victimhood and made themselves into an outrageously aggrieved party. They failed to see, and they truly didn't see it, because they were often brusque in conversation and rubbed others the wrong way, and they indecently exposed themselves to urinate in public. They brought their bodily fluid back inside the establishment to show the minimum wage employee. They could have been charged with assault for this behavior. They couldn't even see the employee wasn't allowed to let customers use the "employee" restroom because of insurance purposes.

This relative I simply pray for. They cannot see that they could possibly be at fault and probably never will. Some are sicker than others. I now offer prayer and pity for them and perhaps a gentle nudge toward their behavior where they allow it. Fourth step prayers and all other prayers from the book Alcoholics Anonymous are in their own chapter in the back of the books.

I've been enlightened to some of my own blindness during this process, it helps me avoid being a hypocrite just condemning others for their horrible behavior. When I was getting high every day, I irresponsibly drove around town. My justification was these were prescription drugs, and the doctor didn't take away my license. I drove very poorly, and two totaled cars served as evidence of that fact. I'm blessed I didn't kill anyone. Yet when I'd get pulled over on a weekly basis, and as glossy-eyed as I was, the officer would insist on searching the car, yet I'd still arrive home stunned by this "persecution" from law enforcement.

My wife would ask, "Well, what were you doing?" My reply was usually, "Just being a law-abiding citizen persecuted for no reason." She'd shake her head in amazement at my lack of insight. Today, it's almost funny to me just how obtuse I was. It wasn't funny until I could actually be truthful about my irresponsibility and negligent behavior.

Like my relative, I couldn't see what I couldn't see.

In the Joe and Charlie app, they speak quite a lot about what has become of the 12 Steps. At the beginning of this fellowship, no one had much time dry and sober from drinking, and therefore measurable change wasn't measured in years as it is today. There are those with many, many years sober whose recovery I don't envy. This is also why I'm writing this book approaching only four years of recovery. I want to show that this needn't take ten or twenty years to start feeling better and accomplishing goals. It didn't even take me five years. I was conscientious in my work on these steps. Being diligent with the steps was the key to success, not a set number of years. I don't hail myself as the paragon of virtue, a life expert, or some mystical guru. I can tell you it is possible to be all of those things with dedication and tenacity toward the work of 12 Steps.

I started simply with an outline of the things that made me angry. Like Russell Brand, I started with an outline of people, ideas, and institutions that angered me throughout my life. The list detailed the big things that came up in my head every day.

I categorized the list based on different ages of my life so I could clearly reference the different things that caused anger and resentment through the years.

Time to break out your notebook and start writing. This first part is simply a timeline of people, institutions, and ideas of things that make you angry. Going through in a timeline fashion can help jog our minds toward remembering.

The Work Begins

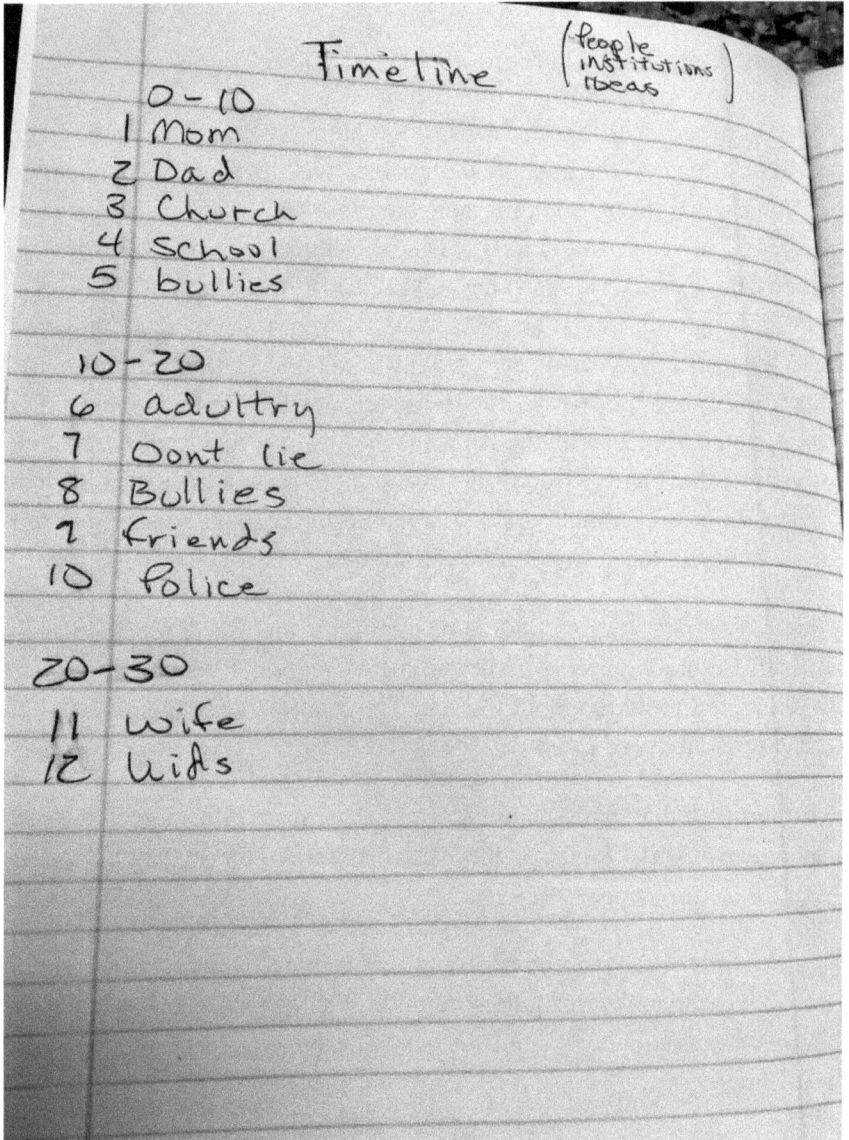

Figure one: We can see to make each part 10 years of our lives: zero to ten, ten to twenty, and so forth.

Next up is an inventory that consists of evaluating and documenting the resentments and their source and impact to identify self-responsibility areas. This is the challenging and rewarding part. It's the final piece of identifying the role we played in the resentment that helps addicts go from being like my family member who is oblivious and impervious to change to being someone who is self-aware, reflective, and growing.

The famous inventory taken from AA directly consists of four columns that should be completed fully one at a time before moving on to the next column.

I'll talk through each of the columns and examples of such before giving you direction to complete your own.

Column One/Resentments: Here, you'll list "all people, places, things, institutions, ideas or principles with whom you are angry, resent, feel hurt, or threatened by."

When I did the inventory, I listed things that really offended me. My mother went on the list. My father went on it. My wife went on it; the children went on it, the idea of adultery went on it, the institution of the church went on it, and the police and government went on it too.

Column One (transfered from timeline)

1 mom
2 dad
3 church
4 school
5 bullies
6 adultery
7 honesty
8
9
10
11
12

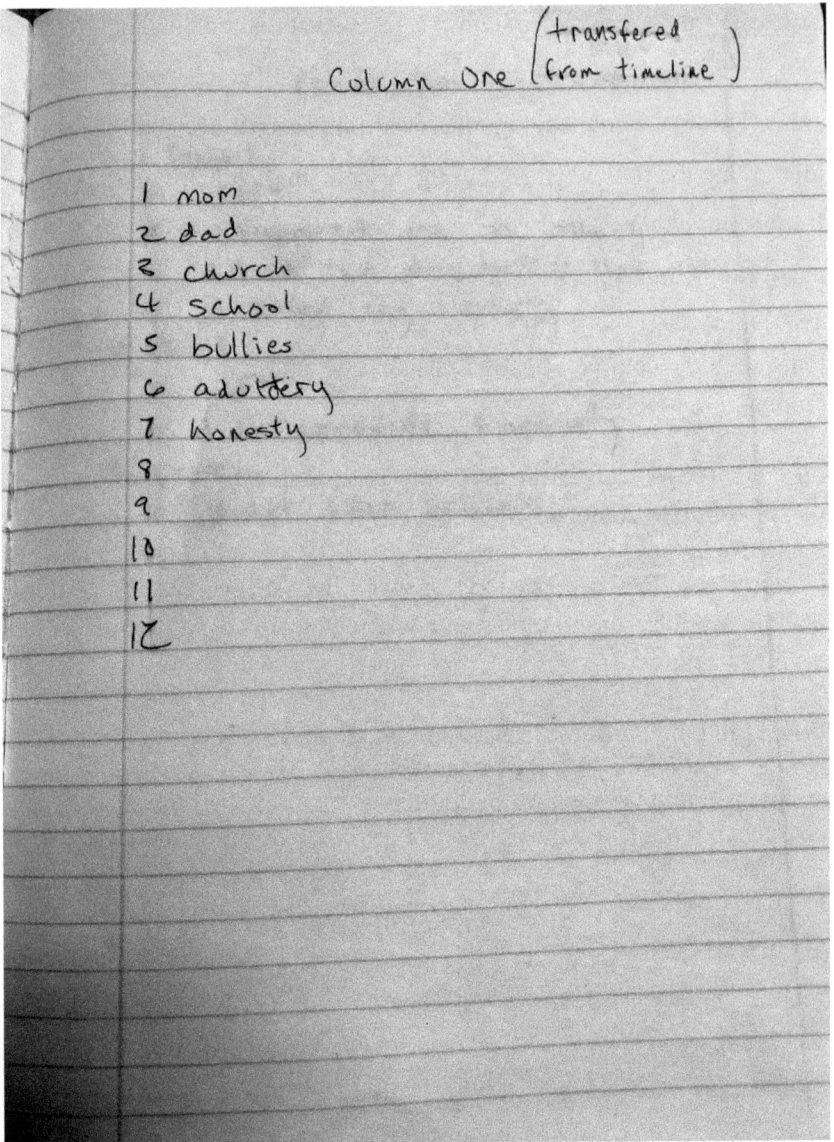

Figure two: Simple transfer into a new column from your timeline. I find numbering to be helpful.

Next, I went on to specific things that made me angry at them individually.

Column Two/Reasons: Here, you'll be specific about why you were angry or resentful of that person or situation listed in column one. It's essential to be clear about what happened and the reason you were angry and resentful.

Here are specific examples from my inventory: My mother left me to live with my grandmother. My wife made me get sober. My kids didn't show me the respect I thought I deserved. The church wanted to control my sex life. The police harassed me. My co-workers told the boss I was drinking on the job.

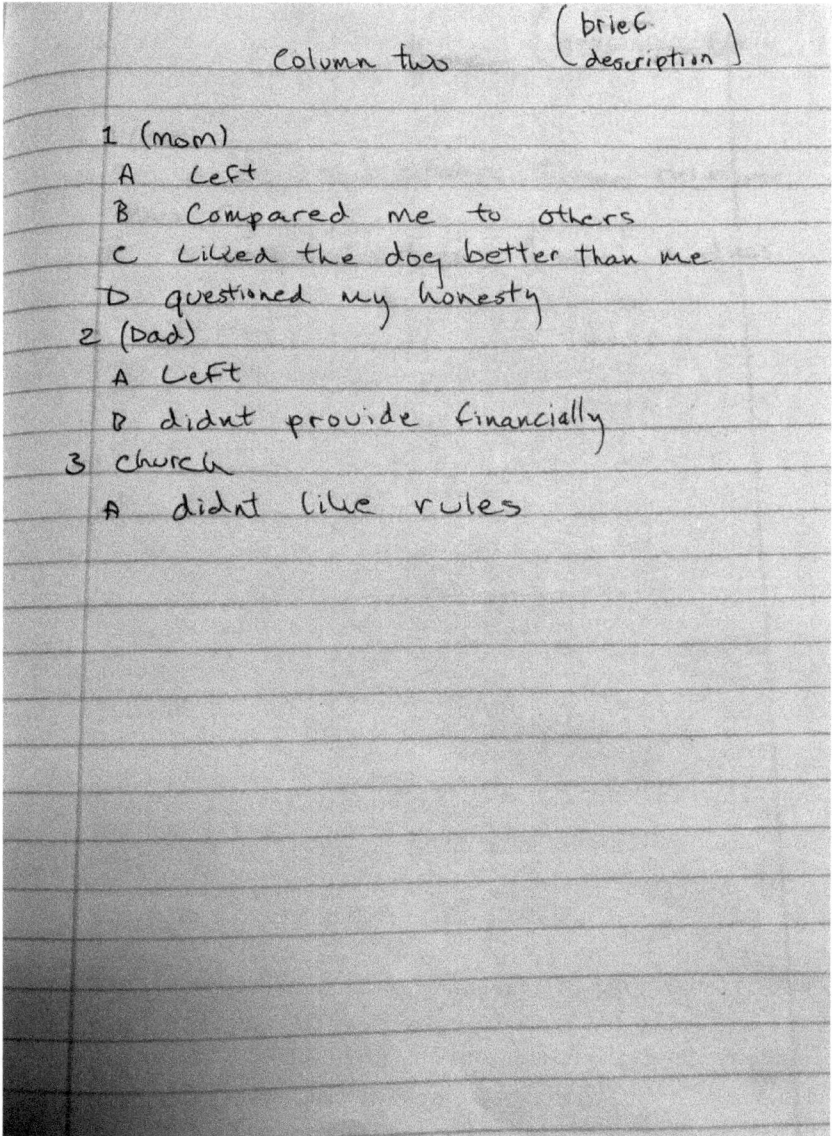

Column two   (brief description)

1 (mom)
A   Left
B   Compared me to others
C   Liked the dog better than me
D   questioned my honesty
2 (Dad)
A   Left
B   didnt provide financially
3 church
A   didnt like rules

Figure three: Brief descriptions of what made you angry. As some have multiple reasons, I use numerals & letters for each individual resentment.

Here are specific examples from my inventory: My mother left me to live with my grandmother. My wife made me get sober. My kids didn't show me the respect I thought I deserved. The church wanted to control my sex life. The police harassed me. My co-workers told the boss I was drinking on the job.

Column Three/Impact to Areas of Self-Affected: You'll evaluate each item and look at how these things affected you and determine their impact on your life. The inventory includes the following questions to help you drill down into the impact:

- How did it make me feel?

- Specifically, how did it affect the seven parts of self:

    o Pride: what I thought others thought of me.

    o Self-esteem: what I thought of me.

    o Personal relations: friendships, co-workers, and general relations with others.

    o Sexual relations: my spouse or others.

    o Security: how I provide myself with food, shelter, and clothing and live.

    o Finances: how my ability to provide for myself and those I loved affected my security.

    o Ambitions: what I dreamed of accomplishing.

Perhaps some of these resentments impacted multiple areas of self.

For my inventory, I asked the questions for each individual resentment. I'll take one of my resentments through the process so you can see what it looks like.

Column One/Resentment: I resent my wife.

Column Two/Reason: My wife made me get sober, which pissed me off greatly.

Column Three/Areas impacted of self:

- Pride: Yes, I wanted her to think I was just grand the way I was.

- Self-esteem: Yes, what she thought of me impacted what I thought of myself, and it made me need to look at the hard choices I needed to make.

- Personal relations: Yes, my wife has always been someone I felt I needed.

- Sexual relations: Yes, my wife is the one I have sex with.

- Security: Yes, she was providing for me and made it clear I couldn't stay in the home while under the influence.

- Finances: Yes, as she provided for me, I was dependent on her.

- Ambitions: Yes, my ambition was to coast on a chemical cloud to death.

Wow! As you can see, the resentment I held toward my wife was a big one as it affected all areas of self. A sponsor was integral during this process of identifying the full impact because at the time I did this, I couldn't even see how some of these areas were affected. I needed more prodding toward honesty, and that is where he would come in handy, nudging me in the right direction.

The next column reveals the part I played in these resentments and problems. We are including fear and sexual misdeeds that caused me a problem here because I think it makes it easier than doing it separately. Others do a separate inventory for sex and fear. Either way is okay. You have done it correctly as long as the inquiry leads you to the promises.

Column three (areas impacted)

1 (mom)
A   pride, self esteem, personal relations, security
B   pride, self esteem, personal relations

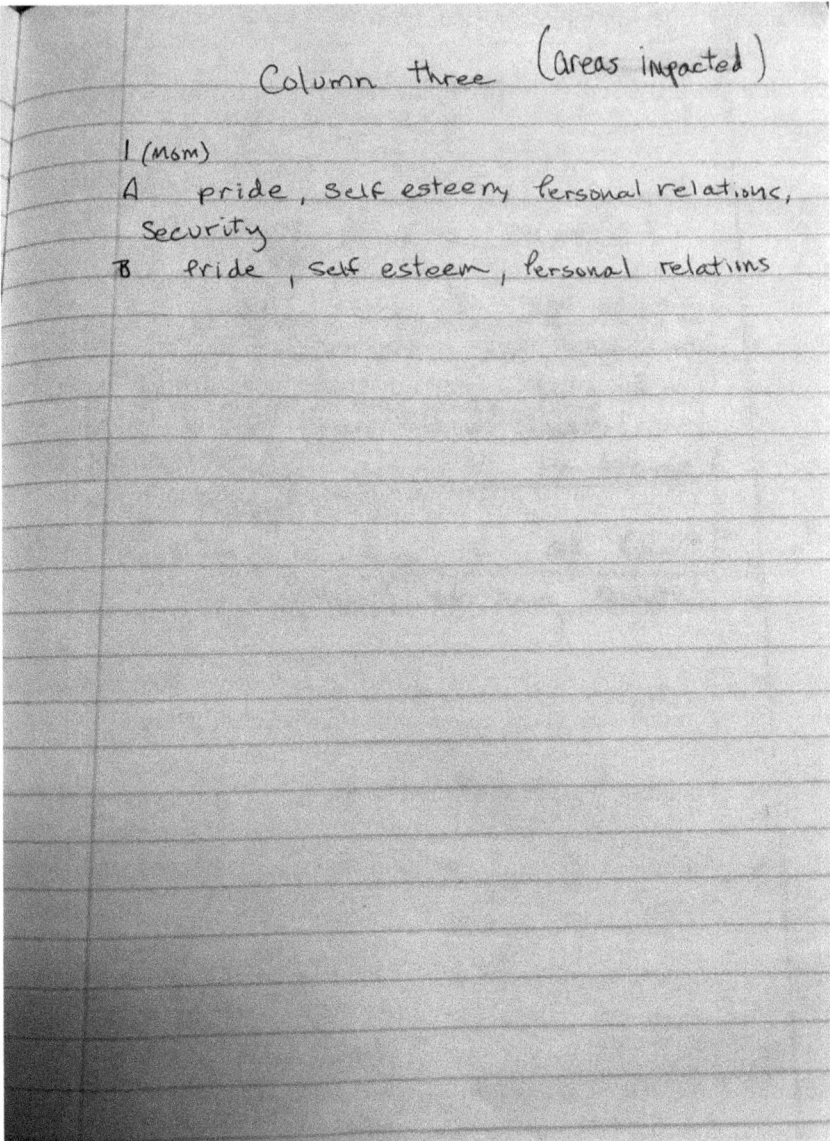

Figure four: Here, I reviewed parts of self-impacted to make me angry. Use the list on the previous page as not all resentments have all parts of self impacted. As you can see, sexual relations, security, finances, and ambitions were not impacted in these two examples.

Column Four/Taking Self-Responsibility: This is where you identify your part in the problem and its impact on your life. It's a matter of identifying where you are to blame. For example, in my process, I realized that I wouldn't be angry for someone telling my wife to put the house in her name had I not been behaving irresponsibly and getting drunk all the time. Again, I asked myself the following questions to derive at the various aspects of my self-responsibility.

Was I mistaken?

My wife wanted the best for me and saw I was destroying myself, and the limits of her tolerance were stretched beyond all her means.

Where was I selfish?

Getting high made me feel at least the semblance of tolerance in my own skin, and therefore I was thinking only of myself.

Where was I dishonest?

It was a giant lie that drinking and using drugs was okay. I was down to 135lbs, and when I didn't have substances, I was panicking. I was irresponsible to the extreme.

Where was I self-seeking?

I sought my comfort first and foremost. Others were always a secondary concern.

What was my fear?

I feared I couldn't live without the substances, as they were the only thing making life tolerable. At the time, this wasn't even a lie because my brain was so obsessed with this comfort.

Where am I to blame?

I had been told many times my addiction was affecting me and those I loved. I justified and rationalized rather than faced the truth.

Where am I at fault?

Faults look at individual character defects. I find the list of the seven deadly sins to work quite well in identifying specific character flaws. The seven deadly sins are pride, envy, greed, gluttony, anger, lust, and sloth.

All of these were affected by the resentment I held toward my wife.

- I pridefully wanted things the way I wanted them and looked toward any excuse to perpetuate my poor behavior.

- I envied those who had wives who tolerated their oblivion.

- I greedily thought of myself first and others second, if at all.

- I gluttonously consumed our resources selfishly.

- I was angry my wife was right.

- I was captivated by lust and didn't want my sex object to leave me.

- I was lazy (slothful) about looking at this predicament.

Where was I wrong? *(This is where we find our amends list or harms done to others) there is a separate worksheet to list these.*

Here's where I found I was wrong:

I was wrong about recovery. I was wrong about my wife's concerns being unfounded. I was wrong about my fear I couldn't live without drugs and be happy. This was proven over time and fellowship, which was a hard-won experience.

I definitely owed my wife a great apology, forgiveness for things she did, and rectifying my past selfish, greedy behavior by working much harder in the future.

It took a great deal of help to do this integral step, and I wouldn't go it alone. I'd find a good mentor or sponsor to help you with this. After reading the chapter on mentorship, you should have some good ideas of where to start looking to find the support you need.

Together, these four columns look like the chart below. I've made several pages of each chart. I believe it's important to do one column at a time to completion before moving on to the next column. I recommend doing the people, ideas, and institutions first and moving on, column by column. A good mentor will be especially helpful when you get to column four and begin looking at your part. Sometimes we become deluded when it comes to the part we played in the chaos. We'll discuss this further when we take the resentments to a fifth step.

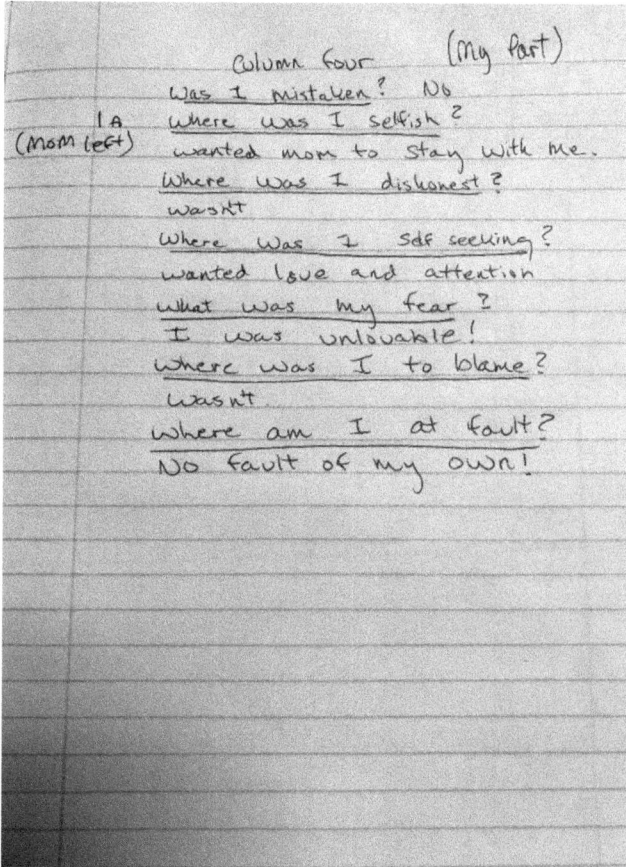

Figure five: I asked these questions for each resentment I had. When I went over these again with my sponsor, I gained more insight. For example, it wasn't wrong as a child to selfishly want my mother's love, but I did carry selfish expectations of love into my adult life, which caused me problems with future relationships. Sometimes the only fault and mistake are using these terrible things to continue our self-destruction. When looking at abuse as children, the only fault is in the story we tell ourselves: we were bad, we liked the attention, and so forth.

I find you really need more room to write, which is why it's hard to do these just using the sheets alone, but they make a handy reference.

FOURTH STEP INVENTORY: RESENTMENTS

				1. Resentful At	2. The Cause	3. Affects My	4. Where was I to blame? (My Part)
				People; Places; Ideas; Institutions	What action was taken that makes me angry/hurt?		
						Self-Esteem	
						Pride	
						Emotional Security	
						Pocketbook	
						Ambitions	
						Personal Relations	
						Sex Relations	
						Dishonest	
						Selfish	
						Self-Seeking	
						Frightened	
						Inconsiderate	
							The Nature of Our Wrong

There are more parts of the inventory to practice: a sex inventory where you used sex selfishly, dishonestly etc., and a fear inventory, but you can glean your fears from the main inventory and evaluate how they held you back. A list of harms done to others can be taken from the inventory where we found ourselves at fault where we had been selfish, self-seeking, dishonest, frightened, and inconsiderate. Sheets to help with these can be found on the internet, and people in your local meetings can help.

This major housekeeping will put you on a path of replacing fear with courage, faith, and resolve to change damaging behavior in your life.

In Step 5, when we share this with another human being, they can tell us when, where, and how our fears are unfounded.

Step 5 "Admitted to God, to ourselves, and to another human being, the exact nature of our wrongs."

You are going to take this inventory to a trusted advisor (sponsor, clergy, doctor) and review it. This should be done with someone who has done it, I believe. I've met many religious and other professionals who don't have a good understanding of this. As I was doing Step 4, I would have questions I'd bring to my sponsor. I'd let him in on bits of truth as we went along. This gave me the opportunity to see if he'd keep my confidences confidential. This built trust. If I got a bad vibe, or he stopped returning my phone calls or picking me up for meetings, I'd have stopped sharing these secrets and found someone else to share this with. While all are experienced with the issues I was writing about, and none were identical, there were enough similarities to identify with. This was supported by my sponsor identifying similar issues. We shared a trust. This is very important as I was so wary of other human beings and had kept so much bottled up inside for fear I'd be hurt or that my trust would be misplaced. So many had hurt me that I was imprisoned in my own mind.

He also helped by gently nudging me toward the truth as he saw it. There was a lot I didn't know that I didn't know. This was the beginning of gaining some insight. This was the start of trusting myself and loving myself—warts and all. I still work on this daily. Problems still arise, as life still happens. People will still let us down and hurt us. Today I simply forgive them. If they are too toxic, I extricate myself from their lives. I no longer dwell in anger, and that makes a big difference.

The confidence I started to feel as a result of doing this work has been amazing. I no longer hate the man I see in the mirror. I actually like and love myself. I experience confidence rather than cockiness arising from the truth. I'm never going to win father or husband of the year. No one is going to mistake me for Eric Clapton when I play the guitar. I deeply know I'm good at my job. I'm good at counseling others with the same problems I've had. I bake a beautiful pie crust. I'm a halfway decent writer. I'm kind of funny. I'm not terrible to look at, though I'm not really very photogenic. Over time, these truths became incorporated into more than beliefs. They became a knowing.

Today I'm on equal footing with my fellow humans. There are no more thoughts of being better than or less than another, which is truly freeing. I'm equal. Next, I needed to remove the rough edges, learn to be kinder, more honest, more charitable, and start practicing more virtuous behavior that lined up with feeling comfortable in my own skin. I also needed to forgive those who injured me before making amends and apologies.

Those deep dark secrets I once harbored are no longer deep or dark. I can openly admit to my past behavior, knowing it was wrong, and understanding why I did what I did. Every single day, I practice not repeating those harmful actions. After practicing this and writing out the fourth step, you'll eventually get used to doing it well enough you'll be able to run through it in your head, which is part of step ten. More on that later.

"Forgiveness has nothing to do with absolving a criminal of his crime. It has everything to do with relieving oneself of the burden of being a victim—letting go of the pain and transforming oneself from victim to survivor."

—C.R. Strahan

CHAPTER TWELVE

Forgiveness

The fourth and fifth steps are for leveling out your ego and your voices that scream, "I am," "It's all about me," "I want," and "Gimme." Settling the ego's drive is done by looking at what offends us, what angers us, what really gets our goat, and what pisses us off. Anger is an umbrella emotion and the bodyguard of fear.

When boiled down, it becomes pretty simple. I'm always angry because I'm either not going to get what I want, or I'm going to lose what I already possess. I'm not going to break down the columns used by *Alcoholics Anonymous*, as there are already many great resources for this. The book *Alcoholics Anonymous* is best used with someone who has been taken through the steps this way. It can be a little murky to guide yourself through a fourth step, never having done one with this book alone. As mentioned in the chapter on mentors, a good guide is integral to understanding what's needed in these crucial steps. The Joe and Charlie app takes these steps apart very well, and even Russell Brand's book, *Recovery*, does a fine job looking at the logistics of these steps. I will write about what I don't see practiced enough or haven't seen enough written about that I found very necessary in completing these steps. This chapter is on forgiveness because I haven't seen any way better to get over my anger toward those who wronged me.

When I began working on this step, I had been isolated for so long in my addiction that I didn't have to write notebooks full of resentments. I had only a few large ones which required an honest look. This work is an individual process. My sponsor couldn't believe I only had a few major resentments because he had so many. I beefed up my list by putting some things that had bothered me in the past but no longer really troubled me any longer. Looking back, I see that this was disingenuous on my part, but I still was a people pleaser and respected this man who was helping me. I also wanted to get this right because I had tried everything else.

Another reason I may have had so few resentments is that in the year leading up to my journey into recovery, I had Electroconvulsive Therapy (ECT). Yes, I had my head shocked to alleviate my major depression after I had tried every other avenue to feel better. ECT dulls out many memories and may be why I had so few giant resentments. The ones I had were big enough, though. I resented my wife and children for pressuring me into getting sober. I resented my mother for abandoning me. Admitting I resented my own wife and children, whom everyone else told me facilitated my way into recovery, was difficult.

Everyone was saying how I should be thanking my lucky stars for having such a supportive and loving family. Saying I resented them made me feel like some kind of psychopath, and in my anhedonia, my behavior and feelings were quite a bit psychopathic.

I think we level up into honesty when we are questioned on how honest we are on subjects. It's helpful when people we trust to point out where we are being hypocritical and are not even aware of the hypocrisy. This attention is never comfortable. Usually, my first reaction to having my honesty questioned is once again anger. I think, "Who the hell are you to question my honesty? Don't you know who I am?" Once again, the ego has been offended. That's all the ego seems to do—get offended and make inordinate lists of daily demands it would like filled. My ego tells me to accomplish more, eat more chocolate, and have more sex. If I accomplish all these childish demands, it will have even a more significant list of demands for me tomorrow.

Fulfilling the ego's demands is never the path to happiness. The ego is like a greedy, entitled child that lives inside of me. Gratitude helps this process;

Paul Moore

as I've written in subsequent chapters, wanting what I have is more important than getting what I want. Needing to get what I want will never be fulfilled. Someone will always have more, bigger, better, faster, and more expensive displays of opulence.

I have developed my path to forgiveness slowly over time. Forgiving my mother, who could easily rile me up every time I saw her, was a long process. In the morning, when I would pray, I'd include her in my prayers. I'd simply ask for her health and happiness and wish her well. Some things occurred as I did this every day for quite a long time. The first thing happened about a month into praying for her daily. I'd see my mother and not get physically stressed out; my shoulders wouldn't tense, my neck and brow wouldn't tighten, nor would my jaw. My stomach wouldn't churn with pent-up anger. The bodily sensations would return if she got on my nerves for a while, so the work was far from complete. The progress was encouraging, though.

I continued to pray daily for her wellbeing, and a few months later, the next part settled in. I started to understand how hard her life was, what she had been through, and the fact that she didn't harbor ill will or bad intent because of her actions. She lived a very hard life herself; she had been abandoned by her mother and raised by her stepmother. She was treated like the proverbial red-headed stepchild. My grandmother had softened by the time she raised me, so I didn't see it, but there was no reason to believe from witnessing their relationship she'd ever really been soft on my mother.

Somewhere around nine months of praying for her wellbeing, I just forgot to include her in my prayers. What she had done, I accepted. I now could spend hours with her without being angered. I remembered the good things she'd done for me. She'd take me to the beach and take me out to eat when she could. For the first time ever, I could see her the way others did. While she still was quite capable of behaving selfishly, she was now a human being to me. When she occasionally did become too much to handle, I'd leave the situation. I understood that changing her was not something I was capable of doing. I can only change myself and how I choose to react to those situations.

I didn't forgive my mother because she earned it. That remains questionable in my eyes. I forgave her mostly because I wanted to feel comfortable in my skin. The forgiveness was more for me than it was for her. The forgiveness was in part in the hope of showing myself and my children how to treat a sick person with love in their sickness. It was doing onto others as I'd have done to me. I recently thanked my mother for giving me this wonderful gift of life. Today I'm capable of doing for her because it's part of my character to be kind and loving—regardless of what she has and has not done.

I've learned that understanding is the key to forgiveness. Statements like "I wouldn't do that, so how could they?" were not conducive to understanding why a person did what they did. This kind of statement is sitting in judgment, and with my behavior toward those who loved me and humanity in general, I wasn't qualified to sit in judgment of others. I'll leave that to something more loving and understanding than myself. I've heard stories of forgiveness for horrible things where the perpetrators didn't deserve forgiveness. But as the fact remains that those people could still bother me even if they were not present in my life, I knew I needed forgiveness for my purposes. Those who injured me never needed to know I had forgiven them. Forgiveness for personal preservation was one of the first virtuous concepts I started to practice. More would come as I went to steps six and seven, and they'd continue to ease my mind and set me on a path of peace. I'd need this forgiveness to be in place, especially when I'd embark on the amends process where I needed to ask for forgiveness for my own shortcomings while not looking at what others had done in response to my behavior.

"He that does good to another does good also to himself, not only in the consequence but in the very act. For the consciousness of well-doing is in itself ample reward."

—Seneca

CHAPTER THIRTEEN

Practicing Virtue

(steps six and seven)

The Paradoxical Commandments

by Dr. Kent M. Keith

People are illogical, unreasonable, and self-centered. Love them anyway.

If you do good, people will accuse you of selfish, ulterior motives.

Do good anyway.

If you are successful, you will win false friends and true enemies. Succeed anyway.

The good you do today will be forgotten tomorrow. Do good anyway.

Honesty and frankness make you vulnerable. Be honest and frank anyway.

The biggest men and women with the biggest ideas can be shot down by the smallest men and women with the smallest minds.

Think big anyway.

People favor underdogs but follow only top dogs. Fight for a few underdogs anyway.

What you spend years building may be destroyed overnight. Build anyway.

People really need help but may attack you if you do help them. Help people anyway.

Give the world the best you have, and you'll get kicked in the teeth. Give the world the best you have anyway.

I read Dr. Keith's paradoxical commandments in a book by Dr. Wayne Dyer. They focus on living by values even when said values are inconvenient for us. I've heard love described as "You love as much as you're willing to be inconvenienced for another person," and this definition stuck with me. Dr. Keith wrote these commandments in a booklet in his sophomore year at Harvard University. He had written about finding purpose and value even when you've not received them from the outside. At such a young age, he had written about one of the archetypes Carl Jung spoke of: the archetype of the spirit. Though most nowadays don't arrive at this archetype, I see vapid surface individuals carrying the realm of the ego onto death. Those who've worked hard at the attribute of being in this archetype are characterized by their inner peace. As my friend Joe says, they have realized, "They are riding a flesh suit on the planet earth."

The flesh suit contains a spirit. When we act in a manner conducive to our spirit, we thrive. It can be hard to discern what this looks and feels like because our ego is a story to the world of who we are. The ego is concerned about outward appearances and things like our accomplishments, talents, physical bodies, and selves. I had a very wise man who repeatedly asked me, "Who is Paul?" His name was Richard Olsen, and he spent many years sober away from alcohol after it nearly destroyed him. He'd ask, and although I'd answer, my answers never seemed to satisfy him.

I'd answer, "I'm Paul. I'm a musician, a scholar, a father, a husband, an employee, a sex god," and other things I told myself about who I was. The correct answer always seemed to allude me, and he never once gave me the correct answer. Instead, he told me I'd know it when it came. Not knowing the "right" answer caused me unending frustration because I told myself I was smart and should be able to glean what he wanted to hear from me. During this time, in my mid-thirties, I was a human doing, not a human being. It took me almost another twenty years and Richards's death in the interim to finally understand what he was getting at. Had he given me the answer rather than it come as an epiphany, I'd not have understood it. I finally understood that I was a soul inhabiting a body, the kingdom of Heaven was within me all along, and I'd never recognized it.

I wondered how admirable people were any different than me. I always admired those who chose to do the right things, and yet they were baffling to me. There were always ladies and gentlemen who selected right over easy and right over feel good right now. There are people who didn't lie, cheat or steal. There are people who return the extra money a clerk accidentally miscounted. Those who'd take a loss financially in business rather than cut a corner. Those who chose self-sacrifice for doing right by their families. How did they do this, and for what purpose? When I started doing the right things like the examples above, they didn't come naturally to me. After all, so many of the wrong things will give us a little thrill, stroke our egos, and make us momentarily happy. Though, the lasting effects of doing the wrong things are guilt, shame, and remorse. Eventually, I realized that the payment for wrong actions was not worth the debt they took from how I felt inside.

I worked with a man who reveled in his character defects, his sin, so to speak. Sin is an old English term that I believe comes from archery, meaning off the mark. In this light, sin is simply a situation where we are a little off course. In the revelry of his off-the-mark behavior, he wasn't happy. He had to continue his lying, cheating, and wrath and justify his actions constantly. I'd wager these justifications fell short of even being believable to himself because he forever needed to justify. When my actions are correct, and in line with my soul, no justifications are necessary. I know my intent, and I'm at peace with it.

Well, this man's justifications eventually ran out, and he was finally fired from his job. He was in recovery with over ten years sober, prayed, and believed in a God quite devoutly. Yet he never started living virtuously. In spite of his recovery, he went about doing the wrong things, asking for forgiveness but never analyzing or making any changes to his behavior. He was abrasive to all he came upon, and many people quit their jobs because they couldn't tolerate his nonsense. I tolerated him for quite some time because I'd learned how to get along with difficult people. I forgive them and show them love. Also, when he'd discuss politics or anything he had an opinion on that wasn't important to me, I'd simply let him be right. My behavior toward this man was much like my friend Richard never told me the answer I was searching for. He simply loved me and let something higher lead me there. In this way, Richard was a conduit of the spirit of God.

The least used action step of the twelve steps.

I once thought meditation was the least used part of the twelve steps and have re-evaluated it. I think the least practiced step is working on your character defects. The book *Alcoholics Anonymous* doesn't expound much further on this subject besides a prayer, and Bill Wilson discusses it further in *The Twelve Steps* and the *Twelve Traditions*. Still, not many people who profess to work the program do much work on character defects. Most get to a level of comfort that is acceptable to them and stop there. If you want to be happy and really comfortable, you won't put your foot on the brakes at these steps. Even after the major housecleaning we've done in steps four and five, more work is usually needed to get really comfortable. This work will be applied in the daily tenth step of looking at the course of our day and seeing where we were off the mark. Did I take that extra five the clerk miscounted, giving me my change? Did I flirt in such a way I'd be ashamed if my wife heard it? Did I lie because it was simply more convenient? Perhaps that clerk is working to support their family, and his counting error cost them their job. Perhaps your wife does hear of your shameless flirtation, and it hurts her feelings, and maybe my convenient lie digs me into a deeper hole as lies often do. But perhaps there are no consequences or are there anyway. Buddhism speaks of karma, and so do most major religions. You reap what you sow, and you measure what you mete.

For me, these seemingly inconsequential bad acts added up to me not feeling very good about myself. I learned that for my self-esteem to thrive,

I need to act right. If I'm okay with being good enough and just not drinking, using substances, gambling, using porn obsessively, or any number of symptoms of the real problem, I can stop changing. Russell Brand describes recovery as paddling a canoe above a waterfall. If we stop paddling, we don't stay where we'd like, and we go backward. I've also heard it described as climbing the down escalator. If we stop climbing, we go backward. Or we might stay sober and miserable, infecting all those we care about with our misery.

Practicing Values

Here we have a list of some more commonly held values, this list is by no means a complete one. I'm sure you can think of some more original values you hold near and dear to your heart. I remember being so out of it while I was reviewing values in one rehabilitation clinic, that when the subject of values came up, I couldn't even remember what they were, never mind any I had. Not one of us is perfect in the practice of any of these values. The goal should just be a competition with who we were yesterday. Just because no one can ever measure up to perfection is no reason to not seek improvement. Practicing our values and improving on them builds good self-esteem. Remember the goal is improvement when we have a bad day and don't measure up to our own standards, we simply forgive ourselves, apologize if needed, and try to not repeat the same mistakes.

Finding our core values and practicing these on a regular basis can help to give us purpose in our lives. I've found the best example of contented sobriety are individuals who have found a good purpose to life that includes helping others. I define contented sobriety, or recovery as having tranquility, serenity, and equanimity; these people are comfortable enough in their own skin to not want or need to use a substance to escape. There are many ways to be of value. It could be running a country, or simply paying someone an appropriate compliment. Holding a door for someone, picking up a piece of trash, or just using manners, are easy ways to increase your value, and as this accumulates your self-image and esteem is improving.

Accountability	Etiquette	Knowledge
Adventure	Fairness	Leadership
Authenticity	Freedom	Learning
Balance	Forbearance	Love
Beauty	Forgiveness	Loyalty
Bravery	Fortitude	Optimism
Boldness	Friendships	Recognition
Compassion	Fun	Respect
Challenge	Generosity	Responsibility
Charity	Growth	Security
Chastity	Honesty	Self-Respect
Citizenship	Hope	Social Connection
Community	Humility	Spirituality
Courage	Humor	Stability
Creativity	Imagination	Status
Curiosity	Industriousness	Tact
Determination	Integrity	Thoughtfulness
Diligence	Intelligence	Transparency
Diversity	Joviality	Tranquility
Equanimity	Joy	Wealth
Equality	Justice	Wisdom
Equity	Kindness	

Journaling prompt: What are the values you hold near and dear they needn't be on the list?

_____

_____

_____

_____

_____

_____

_____

_____

_____

Our character defects.

The simplest look at our character defects is to look into the seven deadly sins. They are: pride, envy, greed, gluttony, anger, lust, and sloth. Though not biblical, I'd add dishonesty as well. People say you can't be honest all the time and ask, "What if grandma buys me a gift I don't like?" Well, I'd say be creative and say something like, "These socks will come in very handy, grandma, thank you." In his book, *The Brothers Karamazov*, Dostoyevsky said this about the impact of dishonesty: "Above all, don't lie to yourself. The man who lies to himself and listens to his own lie comes to a point where he cannot distinguish the truth within him, or around him, and so loses all respect for himself and for others. And having no respect he ceases to love."

Conversely, we have the seven cardinal virtues that are the opposite of the seven deadly sins and have made me feel comfortable with my behavior. Even if I'm not perfect in the application, I'm striving toward perfection. The virtue to combat pride is humility, envy can be met with kindness, the virtue for gree is charity, gluttony can be counteracted with temperance, anger is offset by patience, lust is balanced by chastity, and sloth equalized diligence. With these virtues, we have the ideals to seek a higher goal, and when we work to utilize them, self-esteem starts to form; realizing these goals come from a higher source will keep us humble about the whole thing.

This isn't an all at once revelation or change. You will see certain things crop up even after doing a major housecleaning, as was done in Step 4. For instance, I still get angry if I'm treated unjustly, or I can get irritable in traffic. Sometimes family members who still don't respect what I'm doing or have accomplished can be a source of irritation to me. TWhen this happens, it brings up more forgiveness, tolerance, and love. I was passed over for a much-deserved promotion at work, and I was already doing the job I wanted to be promoted to; because of some bad judgments on the part of my employer, they decided to change the requirements of the position. I didn't like having to audition for a job I was already doing and had achieved great results. I got angry. I sat in this anger for the better part of a day. Did the anger make them instantly give me the new position? No. Did the anger make me a fun person to be around? No. Did I feel comfortable while sitting in the anger? No. Because these were all big negatives, I meditated that night and asked for a solution. The solution presented was a man I didn't know in the emergency room who needed help that I could provide. Helping this man took me outside me. I also felt better and felt reassured I was doing what I was supposed to be doing. After this, it was easier to forgive my employer for what they had done.

I can tangibly feel this forgiveness even if it's not spoken of to those who have wronged me. Because I've forgiven them, I can meet their eyes when I speak to them next. I can apologize and note that I was angry, even when they were wrong. I can be of service to them if and when they ever realize they may have been wrong. If I still hold a grudge, these people will never turn to me for help. But, if I have shown them love and compassion in their error, I become available to help them out of their errors. This is where we start developing faith. We gain insight as we get through little trials and learn from the process. What did I learn from being passed over for promotion? After all was said and done, I had confirmation I was doing what I've been called to do, and I could become helpful even to those who harmed me. Next time, if there is a next time, I'll have the foresight to probably not get as angry if I still get angry.

What are some areas you need to work on? What small things on a daily basing can you do to improve in these areas? How can you serve other people? These small things are random acts of service to our fellow man. Following are some of the little things I needed to practice to understand how those I admired performed admirably. Holding a door open and not getting resentful if they forget to say thank you, or at the very least not giving a sarcastic "You're welcome!" to alert them of the error of their ways. Give the clerk back the extra money, even if you got back to the car and had a debate in your head about it. Speak your truth in a kind and loving manner. Drop your pride and leave your own home to avoid a fight.

Take some time to write even little areas of irritation where you have room for improvements. Also, write down some places where you got it right during your day.

_____

_____

_____

_____

_____

_____

_____

_____

_____

_____

_____

_____

_____

_____

_____

_____

_____

_____

_____

_____

_____

_____

_____

_____

Our eventual goal should be perfection. I'm not saying any of us ever becomes perfect. Challenges will present themselves to the best practicer of these principles. No matter how good we get at practicing these principles, we will never be perfect. Yet we can try, and I've found in trying, I have a far more comfortable existence. Some days my most significant decision is what I'm going to eat that day. Remember, we can slide backward if we don't seek improvement and development in our spiritual lives. Since we have usually lived in turmoil for a significant part of our lives, our backsliding can be imperceptible and slow. Perhaps a friend notices we haven't been helping out the way we once did. If we get angry, they notice it's something indeed to consider. Others can often notice these things before we do, especially if they are also insightful. Sometimes this comes from someone we wouldn't expect and can even present itself as hypocrisy. That can even be true. Even when others cannot see the fault in themselves, they see it in us, and yes, we still should look at it. Perhaps that person's observation will save us from backsliding even more.

Purpose

As I have practiced these new virtues, I've gained a new sense of purpose. Pretty early on in my recovery, I knew my purpose was to serve. It didn't matter how I served. Some of these tasks were menial in nature but not unimportant. Without the kitchen crew at my work, the clients wouldn't eat. Sometimes the leadership or counselors put themselves on pedestals, but without the housekeeping department, the rooms wouldn't be ready, and hence, no clients for them to help. Greeting people at the door of a meeting was one of the first jobs I had in the fellowship. It didn't seem to be a big deal or important role, but it was. I'd do my best to remember people's names and I could see when someone was new and needed help. I could offer to find them a seat and bring them a beverage if they were still shaking.

I remember going to a meeting one of the times I got a little dry time. I arrived magically because I didn't even know where I'd find a meeting and had no list of where to go. I was driving by churches at the appropriate time and saw a lot of cars and guys outside smoking and drinking coffee and decided to take a chance. One day sober, I was miserable after a bad drinking spree. I couldn't meet another person's gaze. When I walked in, someone greeted me. We exchanged pleasantries, and he directed me to have a seat and a cup of coffee. The miraculous part for me happened the next day. I returned to the same meeting, and the gentleman at the door said, "Welcome, Paul; glad you are back." I didn't think I was of any inherent human value or worth. Everyone was angry with me. No one wanted me around because of my drunken behavior. Yet this man, who I can't even remember his name or face, found it important to remember mine. He had valued (loved) me enough to remember my name. This taught me the importance of this very simple act.

Not all important things we do will have important titles but do them anyway. Not every act will give us recognition but do them anyway. We do them not for recognition. We do them because of how they make us feel inside. These seemingly simple acts of kindness will provide the purpose for doing them, even when no other purpose exists. Like Dr. Keith's paradoxical commandments at the beginning of the chapter, even if people will tear down, we should still build. Building and moving forward in small ways gives us the value to continue. I believe that comes from a loving God seeing me behave in accordance with His will.

"It's not a persons mistakes which define them - it's the way they make amends."

—Freya North

CHAPTER FOURTEEN

Making Amends

I just got off the phone with my sister; her mother passed away. Long story short, I didn't grow up with my sister, nor did we really have any kind of relationship for most of our lives. I didn't know I even had a sister for the first fifteen years of my life. There wasn't much contact through my active addiction, and we reconnected just before I started my recovery journey and have kept in touch since. I didn't know her mother except by name and have had no contact with my father since I was fifteen. I reached out to him through his sister, my aunt, and let it be known I held no grudges if he wanted any contact with me. That was some four years ago, and I've never heard back. I didn't want anything from him. I didn't want him to feel like he had to give or burden him, so I left the ball in his court. I harbor no resentments for him and don't even really have a clear story of his part in deciding to have to part in my life.

My mother wasn't the most stable person. She had me very young and was ill-equipped to raise me. My grandmother was my primary caretaker, and my mother would come and go. I had many realizations in recent times of how this abandonment affected me even to this day. For most of my life, I'd seek out those who were unavailable to me and try to earn their love. This epiphany took quite a lot of digging before it came up and bit me on the ass when I realized I was still carrying this behavior into my day-to-day existence. I'd sometimes take things beyond what I needed to in trying to help friends who had no interest in being helped. At fifty-something years old, I was still trying to earn love. It was a hard habit to break, but I had to let certain people go and realize I was not that powerful.

It gets easier once insight and understanding set in and we can forgive people for being human. Today my mother and I still don't have much of a relationship, yet I can still be grateful she gave me life. I've told her this. I tell her I love her often, and I do things for her that are loving. I cook her food and deliver it and drive her to her appointments. Though she hasn't changed much, she's softened up in her age and was a good grandmother to my children. But she is still mostly the woman who chose not to raise me, very selfish and self-centered.

And yet I can tolerate her, be around her, invite her for dinner—without getting flustered and angry while she smooths over the past with a delusional thinking process. I don't know if what I feel for her today is actually love, but it is loving. I have healthy expressed boundaries today, and when she obtusely crosses those boundaries, I forgive her, and if it's too much to take, I extricate myself from the situation abruptly.

Why do I choose to be loving to one who squandered their chance for a good relationship? It's golden rule time: doing unto others as I'd have done for me in a similar situation makes me feel of value. It also demonstrates to my children how to treat an emotionally sick person. In forgiving my mother, I gained insight into what my kids would need to forgive for us to have a good relationship. I really looked further into those relationships and developed them further. I stopped making excuses about what was done to me, and I turned out okay.

As with all areas of the twelve steps, this requires deepening thought as you go along. What served as amends in the beginning changed as I got better. What I apologize for these days is much less than my requirement to give an apology for in the old days.

My desire to apologize is especially true with those I love the most, like my wife, children, and friends. When I first came in, I'd only apologize if I cursed at another person or if I told them "to go fuck themselves" or something similar. These days, I'll offer an apology even if I'm cross, argumentative, or irritable.

Paul Moore

There are many too who are pre-forgiven. Those I love may do something to me in irritation or lack of insight, and they are forgiven without an apology. Sometimes they cannot even see that an apology might be necessary. That's okay. I love these people and forgive them automatically. If they don't realize the importance of an apology, I visit it at an appropriate juncture to talk about.

Though I've never met my sister face to face, nor did I know her mother, I offered to fly out to be with her during this time. I made this offer because this is how I'd like to be treated by those I love. It would also be very cool to embrace someone who is made half of the same genetic material as me.

It's important to have at least some forgiveness for those we make these initial apologies to. Going into this step still holding a grudge for what they may have done to us or what we see as instigating our bad reactions, can cause more trouble in an area where we are trying to get some peace of mind. If I'm still pretty angry with those I should make amends to my body language could tell them something different than my words convey. Even worse, I could blow up on them during the amends process and therefore have something else to apologize for. I prefer not to need amends for my bad amends. I have done this, and it's not pretty. I've given a resentful begrudging apology, and it wasn't well-received. Upon further analysis, I needed to realize the error of my ways, get some new insight, and apologize again.

The amends encompasses more than just an apology in many cases. Some of us, myself included, have stolen time from employers, family, and friends. For employers, these actions are akin to stealing money when I showed up hungover or under the influence. Perhaps even taken more overtly. Some of these amends go under not being made because they could harm those innocent of the offenses. Perhaps admitting all these things to a former employer or person kills my ability to earn a living now and will harm my family. I certainly do not want to cause further harm to those I love and have been irresponsibly deprived of the greatest resource I could give them—myself, my time, my love, and other gifts.

I've developed my own strategies for making amends to some of those people I deprived that it wouldn't be good to reach out to. I give a lot of money to charities and people I see in need. Some think of giving money to those on the street corner as enabling. They have the right to this opinion, but I don't share it. I see giving them this money and having a conversation with them as perhaps instilling their humanity and inherent human dignity. I don't know exactly how God works, but enough great teachers are out there saying, "love one another." I consider my chartable gifts as love—regardless of what they choose to do with the money.

Sometimes bringing value to others, even strangers, to make these amends is the best I can do. Picking up some trash, taking the time to listen to another's problems, holding a door open, and any simple act of human kindness increases my esteem. As I feel better, my state positively impacts those around me, helping make amends.

We get an idea of who exactly should go on the list when we do our fourth and fifth steps. We look at our parts in the wreckage we have caused. If I'm mad that Mr. Smith told my boss I was an addict, because now my boss is looking to see if it's true and effected my ability to put a roof over my head, I still need to look at the fact that the overall cause of my anger was my irresponsible behavior. I've heard some people break this down into columns; if that helps, feel free. They suggest three columns usually labeled the "no way not ever column," the "maybe someday" column, and the "now" column. As time goes by and we are presented with the opportunity, we may move some no and nevers into the now category.

Take some time to write down the people and situations you owe an apology to.

_____

_____

_____

_____

_____

_____

_____

_____

_____

_____

_____

_____

_____

_____

_____

_____

_____

_____

_____

_____

_____

_____

_____

_____

_____

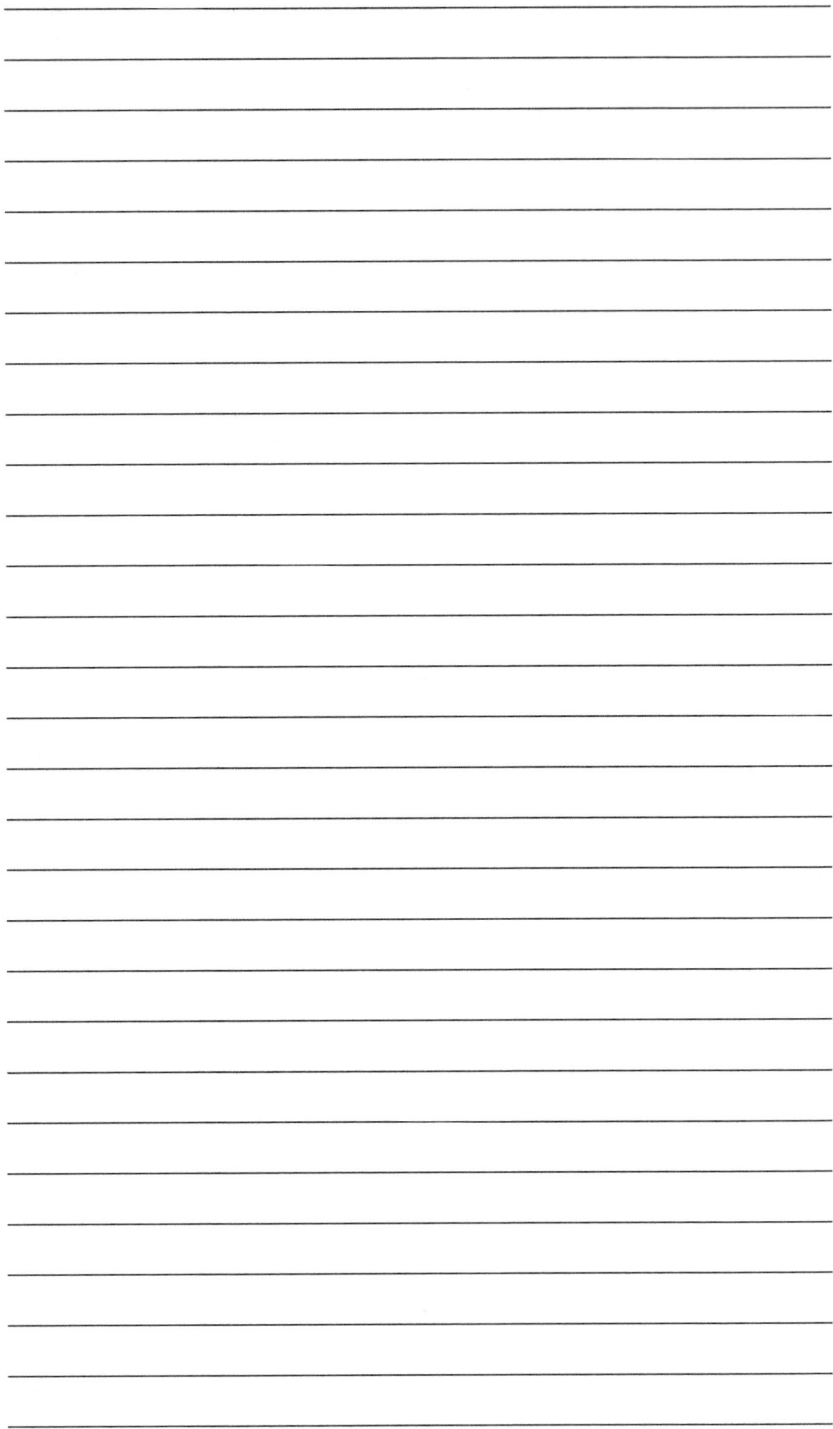

Start of Amends

The start of my amends process probably began prior to complete forgiveness for individuals who had wronged me. I was able to be sincere because I wrote my amends completely and sent them off to those I owed them to. Most of these people were still pretty angry with me at the time because of my behavior. I was at the very least irresponsible toward those I had a responsibility to help and at most negligent in my action toward them. I had embarrassed them, deprived them of emotional security, said hurtful words to them, and most of all, denied them of myself by stealing hours, days, months, and years from them pursuing my addiction.

It was hard at first to realize that taking myself away from them was bad. The fact was I hurt my friends and family members often when I was around them. Because I didn't love or care for myself at all, I didn't know what I was depriving them of. Loving oneself is the beginning of understanding love on a more profound level. When I love myself, I'm more loving to others because I understand and feel love. I believe understanding and feeling self-love is the key to unconditional love. I would do loving acts before, but often they were contingent on the love being returned to me. The more I love myself, the less of a return I need because I already possess it.

With a sober mind, I asked myself, "What do I want for these children I've claimed to love?" With a sober and loving mind, my answer was, "I want the best for them. I want them to have all the good things that exist in the world." Seeing God as a loving father allowed me to love myself because what else would a loving father want for his children other than the best of all things?

I didn't possess a time machine or even a souped-up Delorean, which would take me back in time and allow me to raise my children in the manner I thought they deserved. I couldn't travel back and be the husband my wife should have had, nor the son my mother should have had. I did however love these people and wanted relationships with them. From this point on, I expressed that to them, along with the remorse that I hadn't lived up to my capabilities due to my addiction. I thanked them for not giving up on me and asked for their forbearance and forgiveness.

Continuing Amends

After I made my initial amends and my family started to see changes in me, things in my life started to change. My life transformation didn't occur overnight and is still in process and likely always will be. The destruction of my past left a lot of anger in its wake, and the best way I can teach forgiveness is to demonstrate it myself. I knew forgiveness had taken place for those who hurt me when I could remember the good things in even destructive relationships.

I've outlined this in the chapter on forgiveness. When I couldn't understand the process, I simply prayed for those who hurt me. Forgiveness comes quicker, as I've gained insight over the years. It's easier now to see why a person behaves in a hurtful manner. Most people are selfish and put themselves and perhaps their families first. Self-preservation seems like a good thing, but when used as a reason to justify hurting others, it's still harmful.

I've had things happen in my career that were extremely unfair. I've been passed over for promotions where my qualifications exceeded what was required. I was naturally angry with the decision makers when another with lesser qualifications and capabilities was promoted to the position to which I felt I was entitled. The position I'm in is one they have a hard time filling, and I do it well. I can see their purpose in keeping me in this position, which helps outweigh treating me unfairly. When I can understand they are doing what is best for themselves, however selfish, however unfair, I gain the understanding of why they are doing it. Once I understand and know their decision is not even personal against me, I can adjust my expectations and gain acceptance over the perceived injustice. In the past, I've done these wrongs where I unfairly put myself above all others.

In order to continue the relationship process, I asked some hard questions of those I'd have a continuing relationship with. I asked my adult children if it would be possible to take them out to eat occasionally and find out how they are. This request wasn't met with immediate love and acceptance. Instead, the idea was met with skepticism, as the kids asked themselves, "What does dad want now?" Their response was an understandable reaction to my past behaviors. Did I just give up? The answer is "No." While I didn't want to be bothersome to my adult children, I said I'd occasionally send this offer in a text to let them know I was thinking of them. Sometimes, we have to ask if the small action of a text is even ok or if we are being too intrusive. Some of us have damage that's best left untouched where others may wish to involve the courts. If this is the case, we may have to respect their wishes for no contact from us. By doing this, we have at the least done our part in this process and know we are willing to accept the consequences of our actions. We can pray and meditate on the necessary actions—if any- and be ready to be more direct with amends and take further action if the time ever becomes appropriate.

Living Amends

I've had a lot to amend for just living like a self-centered, selfish person for so many years. I believe these amends to society at large can be made by living right.

Perhaps now I need an extra measure of love and tolerance for people in general. The bonus is love makes me feel good. I enjoy making people laugh and smile. I enjoy giving to those who need assistance. I learn lessons from those still at a different level in their lives. I can practice forgiveness when I am wronged and pardon those who wrong me. I've heard it said that unlimited patience brings immediate results, and I've seen those results regularly. Once these virtues are put into practice, my problems become life-sized instead of overwhelming and impossible to manage. They no longer feel intolerable because I feel one on my side who is all-powerful.

As I practiced more and more, I could even live in joy during the chaos. My moods are no longer controlled so entirely by circumstances. I can now choose to be happy instead of looking for and living in the problems. At first, I practiced patience by simply keeping my mouth closed while I was angry, which wasn't true patience. I eventually became long-suffering the more I practiced, without even getting angry. I can observe this now, as I'm being disparaged and still have equanimity. This ability is more precious than gold to me.

Having had many so-called bad things happen has actually turned out to be a good thing—especially now that bad things are not occurring. Living in my car and being put in prison at least taught me I could survive under even harsh circumstances. What can you do to someone who has experienced their greatest fears and still survived? The answer is "Nothing." I overdosed and was revived by emergency medical technicians, and I came so close to death many times. The result was I lost the fear of death. While I lived in utter pain and lost even my ability to walk for a time, I still survived. When you come back from such grievous losses, you can choose to start appreciating some seemingly small things. Today I'm grateful I can sit still in a chair. I'm thankful I can eat beef jerky without my teeth breaking. I'm happy to eat food from my pantry. I'm grateful I can walk normally again.

These days, I've lost the desire to be special. When I pray in the morning, I pray to have the strength to do His will and to be of service. The funny thing that occurred from looking to be useful rather than to shine is I became special in my usefulness. Whether the task is to help move a sofa or to conduct a group for alcoholics and addicts, I'm useful. It feels useful to make people laugh. It feels useful to listen to someone's problems. I feel honored when those who have been closed down for so long open and share scary things with me. Being useful raises my feeling of self-worth and inherent value. It makes me feel a part of society rather than apart from it. It makes me feel connected, and it makes me feel loved.

Try to journal some of the ways you bring value to others in your life. Items on the list can be very small, like holding open a door, picking up a piece of trash, or giving someone a compliment. These little acts of service are things I've built upon through the years I've been given. The payback for these acts is incredible when you are not doing it for payback. Your brain will release endorphins while you are being selfless. Those who witness your selflessness will get an endorphin rush because of mirror neurons. We might not be able to change the world, but perhaps we make it a better place for even one person.

Paul Moore

Write down the small and large ways you bring value to the world.

_____

_____

_____

_____

_____

_____

_____

_____

_____

_____

_____

_____

_____

_____

_____

_____

_____

_____

_____

_____

_____

_____

_____

_____

"I think that the power is the principle. The principle of moving forward, as though you have the confidence to move forward, eventually gives you confidence when you look back and see what you've done."

– Robert Downey Jr.

CHAPTER FIFTEEN

Aligning Consciousness

Step 10

Steps ten through twelve are often referred to as the maintenance steps. I like to think of these as the growth steps, as I believe a good recovery is one of continuous growth. "You either grow or you go," I've heard spoken by many whom I respect. I believe this is true, and I believe these steps are how we practice daily. Indeed, maintaining a spiritual connection allows us to live comfortably free of our addictions.

Step 10 is the combination of one through twelve each day. I do this now either during the course of the day or at its culmination when I retire for bed. Steps one through three are done when I awaken as I pray. Saying my morning prayers is: admitting I need help (Step 1), believing a power greater than myself can help (Step 2), and asking that power to guide me (Step 3). If I get ruffled during the day, and someone manages to piss me off, I can do a spot check inventory. Now that I've done a complete fourth step, I can run through it in my head. I can always refer back to my guide if I need help or if I have a conundrum. I start by asking, "What did they do?", "What aspect of self did this affect?" "What was my part?" "Where was I selfish, self-seeking, inconsiderate, or afraid?", and "Do I owe them an apology?" If yes, I ought to get that done as soon as possible. I can then call my sponsor, especially if my insight isn't very developed yet.

Sometimes I've had to pull out my fourth step guide to run through a particularly hard problem. I once was confronted by some more old-fashioned members of my group about receiving rides to meetings from a beautiful young woman. In an earlier chapter, I've mentioned the notion of men socializing only with men and women mingling only with women. This is one of those unwritten rules in the fellowship. At the time, I greatly respected many of these men who helped guide me during my time in recovery. I even placed some of them on pedestals. I looked at many in awe of their accomplishments. This is a precarious place to put another human being. After all, we are all human.

Back then, I had no driver's license and had to get rides where I could. I had no untoward intentions for this woman and hadn't acted in an ungentlemanly fashion. When confronted, I became angry because I had asked others for rides and felt they could have offered, especially if they were going to take umbrage at my riding to a meeting with a woman. The member who confronted me also had some old-fashioned, skewed views of relationships. He was even perplexed that a man and woman could be friends without hanky-panky. His assertions spoke volumes about what his own relationships with women were like. In taking his inventory, I saw he never had healthy relationships, and his bias became apparent.

He got in my face and forbade me from riding to the meeting with her. I liked this not at all. Also, as my fears subsided, I didn't acquiesce to his demands. I still respected this man, though that respect greatly faded after this incident. I didn't, however, raise my voice, curse at him, punch him in the head, or do any behaviors I needed to apologize for. So that was a win. I was still incensed about this incident for about two weeks. I rehashed it with my sponsor and others. Certainly, it affected my pride, and I believed it also impugned my character. I also thought there was a better place and a better time for my group member to approach me.

I eventually got out pen and paper and ran the situation through another inventory. Upon doing so, I realized how wide the demands impacted things for me. His view could affect my marriage if a scandalous rumor broke out because of it. It also affected my aspirations as those involved were part of a wider recovery community where I was seeking employment. The discontent touched my reputation too. I didn't want others saying I was some kind of predator. And as it was my safe home group where I felt, until this time, loved and accepted, and I knew returning to substances would kill me, it affected my ability to stay alive.

It took the rewrite to see how deeply this incident affected me. At least I maintained enough decorum that I didn't owe that man an amends. Making amends to an asshole is one of the worst amends you'll ever need to make. I've had to do this occasionally, and it's so much better just to keep my big mouth closed! I eventually found another group and chalked the experience up to some are still sicker than others even if they talk a good game. This man never saw his part in the impact to date, though he professes great insight and is a hale fellow well met in the fellowship.

I took this problem to God in prayer and meditation, prayed to forgive this man, and spoke volumes of it to my sponsor. Through these actions, I learned my reputation is different in everyone's mind. Forty different people will have forty different reputations for me; all of them are none of my business. I and my higher power were in charge of my life, and I could find another group. I also stopped putting people on pedestals and realized all human beings are prone to be fallible. From this point forward, I decided I'd be warier about watching people's actions rather than just hearing their flowery speeches. We can all sound good when we polish our rhetoric. This new understanding completed the fifth step of this incident. Six and seven were looking at where I had been selfish, self-seeking, inconsiderate, and afraid. I feared my life could return to drugs, and I didn't practice faith during this. Steps eight and nine were left out because I maintained the semblance of a gentleman, thank God!

Continuing Practice

Most of the time, it won't be an overwhelmingly large problem like the one I just illustrated. More likely, it'll be an argument with the wife, the boss, or on social media. It is integral though we continue to look at these if we wish to stay spiritually fit. I usually now can reach the end of most days and lay my head on the pillow, and fall comfortably into a restful sleep. I've heard this ability called "the pillow test." If I'm twisting some incident of the day over in my head excessively, I need to evaluate it. I'm probably all set if I'm relaxed and ready to sleep. This continued practice is what brings us into a state of equanimity. We are hardly able to get flustered now in this state. I no longer get upset if someone doesn't share the same view on politics, religion, or life in general. I don't feel the need to correct them. I'm open-minded enough to consider new information that may change my beliefs if they are wrong. Correcting someone or winning an argument is all about satisfying my ego. I do have opinions and will be honest when asked what they are. I can explain them today in a kind manner, and because I can share them freely and easily, they are more likely to be accepted by those even with a different perspective.

I have a friend who is a practicing pagan and Luciferian, while I'm fond of the Buddha, Jesus Christ, and a philosophy of loving your enemies and avoiding material desires. This friend knows all about my views and one day started to proselytize about how my faith is a slave faith. She said it was designed to keep people down and controlled. I could see many of her points, but my faith has led me to happiness so far. The whole time she was going off, I didn't get angry or upset. I didn't try to convince her she was wrong or tell her she was going to hell. After she ranted, I simply asked if I had ever proselytized to her that her beliefs were wrong or inferior. She stopped for a tic and replied that I hadn't ever done that. I told her I never would, as she'd know me by the fruit of my behavior. We are still good friends to this day because this faith has taught me love and tolerance. It has taught me to show people who I am rather than tell them.

Growth Step

Life has gotten easier as I've gotten over some of the more glaring defects of my character. I'm far less stressed, and my usual state is one of peace, happiness, and

serenity. Keeping our stress levels manageable is so important. Particularly when we're stressed, it's easy to drift back into our old patterns. Having those around us who keep us honest and growing is very important. I could build up and juggle many problems during active addiction because I had a chemical crutch. These days, I can do the same thing without needing to spend money, have sex, or binge-watch Netflix. It's important I do not do this; it's important to keep my stresses low and manageable. We are usually the last to see when we are not doing what we are supposed to, but we will feel it. Before we can see the impact, we may become restless, irritable, and discontent. If we operate in this capacity for too long, the liquor store and the drug dealer start to look appealing again.

In summary, we do all the steps every day. The good part is it gets easier, and becomes a habit that we don't have to devote much thought to. I actually got steps 11 and 12 in there too, if you noticed. Thinking (meditating Step 11) on my problem, and I reached out to others for insight (Step 12), allowing them to help me, which I know is a help to them, and, therefore, service. We will get deeper into meditation and service in the following two chapters. The main points of this chapter are as follows:

- Continued growth

- Daily practice

- Equanimity and peace of mind

"When we really keep in the forefront of our thoughts that our intention in this life is to recover and be free, then being of service, practicing meditation, and doing what we need to do to get free becomes the only rational decision. This takes discipline, effort, and a deep commitment. It takes a form of rebellion, both inwardly and outwardly, because we not only subvert our own conditioning, we also walk a path that is totally countercultural. The status quo in our world is to be attached to pleasure and to avoid all unpleasant experiences. Our path leads upstream, against the normal human confusions and sufferings."

— Noah Levine

CHAPTER SIXTEEN

Daily Practices

Step 11

"Sought through prayer and meditation to improve our conscious contact with God as we understood Him, praying only for knowledge of His will for us and the power to carry that out."

Preconceptions vs. what it is.

When I first thought about mediation, my immediate focus went to zen masters sitting under waterfalls, completely at peace without any thoughts troubling them. Next, I said, "I could never do that. My head is like a mess of tangled Christmas lights that never stops." I had the notion ahead of time that meditation just wasn't something I could do. Following is a good time for a quote from the big book by Herbert Spencer indicating what I had before opening my mind. "There is a principle which is a bar against all information, which is proof against all arguments and which cannot fail to keep a man in everlasting ignorance—that principle is contempt prior to investigation."

I had to get over saying I couldn't do something without even trying it, and meditation was one of these things. My earliest meditations were me just quietly ruminating on my front stoop. I'd grab my coffee and watch my cats play on the lawn, look at the blue sky, investigate the leaves on the trees, and take in my surroundings. Go figure this was meditation. I had no idea! It's been practiced by religious people of all types, under many names. Christian monks called this contemplative prayer. The Bible says in Psalms 46:10 "Be still, and know that I am God."

Taken quite literally, this stillness is meditation. Daily meditation practice has changed my life in many, many ways. There are whole books devoted to the science of spirituality. Dr. Rupert Sheldrake has written much on this subject, including how meditation improves our health, immune systems, mental health, intellect, and more. I believe these benefits appear best when meditation is a consistent practice. We need to devote at least a couple of minutes every day to being still. I eventually scheduled a time I'd do it daily, and the practice started showing prodigious results. Combined with being present and mindful, a consistent meditation practice solves problems. Answers would come to me in the meditation I hadn't thought of. Eventually, I revisited some unpleasant areas of my childhood and could look at them as detached, where they didn't hurt as much. I corrected childish thoughts that I wasn't good enough, that I was unlovable, that I was bad. I also realized many who hurt me were not evil. Through meditation, I understood these people were just selfish human beings, which made it easier for me to forgive them.

I've had inspirations arrive during my meditations. Stuff came to me as if out of the ether while I was calm and contemplative. My idea to write a book, start a podcast, and expand my education came from meditation. Instead of being stuck in the past and focused on my problems, I started saying, "Why not me?" when thinking about success. My inner dialogue changed from meditation. While addicted, and for a while afterward I'd still disparage myself. I'd call myself an idiot or a loser. I started changing those scripts in my meditations. When you change your thoughts, you change your feelings. Our brain attaches a feeling to every thought we have—angry thoughts bring about angry feelings, depressing thoughts equal depressing feelings, and happy thoughts produce happy feelings. Happiness had to come from within. It wasn't achievable through some material success. This freed me from myself and the bondage I kept myself in. After I had practiced daily for a while, I was feeling better. The affirmations I told myself got better and doing them while in this altered state of mind quickly rewrote the negative bullshit I once told myself.

Easiest meditation ever:

You can do this. Write down five things that make you happy. Write things that really make you happy, not things we expect to make us happy. For example, I was told having a beautiful family should make me happy, but when the beautiful family wanted me to step up and stop behaving poorly, they didn't make me very happy. These five things could really be anything. I bought a new leather knapsack, and I love how it smells. I love lilacs like the ones that once bloomed in my window as a child. I like my purple phone, and I like my truck. The list is limitless. Find five and write them down. Although I covered this in another chapter, I believe it's important enough to write it twice.

Here's some space to write happy things.

_____

_____

_____

_____

_____

_____

_____

_____

_____

_____

_____

_____

_____

_____

_____

_____

_____

_____

_____

_____

Okay, you've got your happy list. Now, sit or lie down and breathe as deeply as you can into your abdomen. Most adults breathe 16-20 shallow chest breaths per minute because most adults are in some state of fight, flight, or freeze, all their waking hours. If you want, you can count your inhalations and exhalations. Try to exhale longer than you inhale. That's it. You are meditating. This can be done every night as you try to sleep. You are, after all, trying to relax enough to sleep anyway. Devoting five to ten minutes daily to this practice will work wonders for you.

Developing a Conscious Contact

In those quiet moments where my brain stops thinking thoughts is the place I go to experience God. I believe meditation and hypnotherapy work so well because there is a higher power in the mix. Higher powers are the special sauce of these practices. I've tried to lie to myself about my behavior while in these trance-like states, and something keeps me honest. I've brought problems to meditation and found solutions in the stillness. Many times the answer isn't one I want to do. The most frequent solutions require me to feel more, be more forgiving, have more patience, express more tolerance, and share more love. These commands are not my natural way of thinking. Especially when I first started, my mindset was to get even, screw them, and ruminate on negative thoughts like "nobody loves me." Dr. Rupert Sheldrake was an atheistic scientist who found his way to God during meditations. He's got a great YouTube channel where he speaks about it. Testimony of others will only get you so far in this journey. You need to develop this quiet space.

Breathwork

How I breathe has expanded over time. My deep abdominal breathing is my staple to center myself. There are so many techniques out there waiting for you to discover. Wim Hof learned to control his sympathetic nervous system, a feat of skill scientists once said couldn't be done. Hof, known as "The Iceman," has a book, The Wim Hof Method: Activate Your Full Human Potential, detailing his breathing technique, and I've employed some of his suggestions in my breathwork. These exercises let you gain control over your stress response of fight or flight. When you master some control over this, you are calmer, more at peace, easier going, and healthier.

I usually, in a waking state, breathe about four to six times a minute. I've looked at it during my meditation, and it can take about 40 seconds for one cycle of breath (full inhale and exhale). I'm not depriving myself of any oxygen when doing this. My cells use less as I'm in a state of high relaxation. For drug addicts, imagine the effects similar to taking two ten milligrams of Valium. My lung capacity has also significantly increased by breathing deeply and fully into my abdomen. If you watch a baby breathe, they do not do those shallow chest breaths regularly, they breathe deeply into the abdomen. This also relieves pressure on the vagus nerve. The different types of breathwork I've done and their effects are listed below.

4x4 breathing:

This is one where I count four for my inhale, rest for a four-count, exhale for a four-count, and rest for another for four-count. This technique helps if your thoughts are very active in what the Buddhists call the monkey brain. Since you are counting in your head, it's hard to have another thought during the process.

6x6 breathing:

This method is like 4x4, except it's a six-count instead. I've heard this also called heart coherence breathing, which is used to balance the head and the heart. When I do this, I usually tuck my chin to my chest, keeping my spine straight.

Tongue against the roof of the mouth:

A wise master told me of meditation that when we think in words, our tongue makes micro-movements that correspond to these words. He told me to let my tongue rest lightly against the roof of my mouth and imagine a string tied pulling it lightly toward the back of my head. He said this helps to stop the monkey brain. I've done it, and it surely helps.

Wim Hof:

The Iceman has several breathing techniques; I'll not document them here, as he has written a great book documenting them.

Using a mantra:

This technique includes repeating a mantra over and over again, either aloud or silently. I like saying, "Aaahhh," because it requires just opening my mouth. I've found when I chant this vowel sound, perhaps due to its vibration, I feel a sense of calm come over my limbs. I've found this also helps with shutting down the noise chattering away in my head.

Kundalini breathing:

This breathing begins when I tighten my stomach muscles as I breathe in and tighten my pelvic floor, you'll know you are doing it correctly when you feel pressure in your lower back. This combination of breath and tightening pushes cerebral spinal fluid up through the brain, activating your pineal gland, which can release all-natural DMT, a powerful hallucinogen the body makes. When I stretch after employing certain techniques, I get high as a kite. I've illustrated one such technique next. So if you thought you could never catch a buzz again, you were wrong. I'm always excited to share this prospect with other recovering drug addicts who also love the euphoria!

My meditation to get high on my own supply

Tonight I experienced an ineffably euphoric silence at the end of my meditation. I meditated using my newest combination of breathwork, a tone shared by a friend, and a stretch that opened the spine like the downward dog position in yoga. I'm sharing this because I hope you'll have the same experience as it transcends any words I can use to describe it. I've not tried this using my normal meditative soundscapes, so I include this tone from YouTube.

The feeling I had upon my inhalation of breath after the meditative process I'll describe was like no other I've experienced in my time on earth. I reveled in the most beautiful silence I've ever known. The silence was akin to what I imagine Heaven is. I felt not like a body, but like a pure unrestricted spirit, in the presence of pure love and joy. For that moment, I didn't feel like a human who was being a human. I wish mere words could convey this feeling.

The process is similar to the Wim Hof method, with one notable difference at first. In the Wim Hof Method, you take in thirty to forty deep abdominal breaths (I do forty) while relaxing to let the air out, followed by complete exhalation. Upon the exhalation, you refrain from breathing as long as you can. I worked my way up to about a minute and a half by the third set. This action is followed by a full inhalation filling the lungs. I gird and tighten my stomach muscles for the beginning of holding this second breath. This is repeated three times. I alter this by making the first fifteen breaths of the set, stomach tightening kundalini breathing for the three sets. During this breathwork, I also experienced great euphoria.

My next phase goes into about fifteen minutes of Japa meditation, made famous by Wayne Dyer. This meditation involves chanting the long "Aaahhh" sound while envisioning the Lord's Prayer. I make the "Aaahhh" sounds between the words of the first two sentences and continue throughout the meditation. This takes about another 15 minutes. I'm certain this is available on YouTube.

Phase three is leveling up the gratitude and focusing on manifesting my goals. My method of leveling up my gratitude is thinking about the many friends, other healers, and family I'm surrounded by. Sometimes I'll think of old clients who said I made a difference in their recovery process. I simply think about each person and offer them my love and blessings. While I'm doing this, I do 6x6 heart coherence breathing.

I feel like a disembodied spirit by the time I imagine my goals completed to fruition. I do very long visuals of exactly how I want things to turn out. I thank God regularly during this process. Considering the manifestation of my goals takes about another fifteen minutes.

Next, I rest, breathing normally and returning to the sensations of my body. After this, I stretch. I was meditating in a seated position, so I sat up, arched my lower back, and reached forward, bringing my arms up and stretching as far back as possible. While exhaling, I return my arms to my chest and take a great breath of air in. This inhale was magical and different. I usually get a great high anyway, but tonight's was incredible. Talk about getting high on my own supply. I hope you have similar results if you try it.

Prayer

There are many types of prayer to investigate. I try not to be selfish in my prayer. In general, I ask for the strength to do God's will, and I ask to be useful. I say this simple prayer in the morning. At night when I pray, I say thank you for my sober life. When I pray, I'm not usually begging for new cars or scandalous amounts of cash. I'm grateful for what I have and sometimes ask for specificities. If a friend is in poor health, I make a request for their improved health. If I need help solving a particular crisis, I make a request for clarity and a solution. If I'm angry and need to forgive someone, I'll make a special prayer to help me understand them.

If you don't like certain prayers, make up your own prayers, I often chat with my higher power to the point that I sometimes look like a crazy person talking to myself. I say "Thank you" very frequently during the course of my day. When an errant thought arises of how nice an eight ball of cocaine and a handle of whiskey would be, I shoot off a request for the desire to be dismissed. I don't like to entertain these notions as they usually lead me to romanticize the euphoria. I seldom will just recall the complete abject debasement I suffered and imparted on those I love.

There are many breathing, meditation, and prayer techniques. Get creative and write your favorite I've provided space below to do so.

_____

_____

_____

_____

_____

_____

"I think a spiritual journey is not so much a journey of discovery. It's a journey of recovery. It's a journey of uncovering your own inner nature. It's already there."

— Billy Corgan

CHAPTER SEVENTEEN

Spiritual Awakening

Step 12

"Having had a spiritual awakening as the result of these steps, we tried to carry this message to alcoholics, and to practice these principles in all our affairs."

Spiritual awakening, what's that?

Upon reviewing Bill Wilson's story, many early members of Alcoholics Anonymous were wondering where their "white light" conversion moment was. Bill feels this moment came over him like the conversion Saint Paul experienced on the road to Damascus. Sometimes this happens, but you'll likely have one that is of the learned variety. There is a description of this in the back of the big book. A learned experience comes over time, practice, and working the program through the steps. Sometimes it's imperceptibly slow, and we fail to notice it. Other people may notice the change in you before you do. I think of it kind of like going to the gym. If I'm looking in the mirror every day, it's hard to see any change. If someone I haven't seen since I started working out runs into me, they will probably notice there's something different about me.

For me, others were quick to notice how I no longer flew off the handle. They noticed me being honest and doing as I said I would. These days, I show up for work every night a bit early to be considerate of my co-workers' time. I'm far more loving in my regard to humanity in general and want to see others do well.

Some think service only begins when one completes the steps and sponsors others. I think service should begin immediately. The sooner one starts being of service; the sooner one begins to feel better about themselves. There are many ways to give service, in and out of meetings. My service needn't only be for others who suffer from addiction. My service can be any way to make the world a better place. These acts of service include simple things like holding the door for someone, picking up a piece of litter, letting someone into traffic, giving someone a ride to a meeting, listening to someone's story, and sharing my story. Honestly, the list is endless. My goal is to make a better version of the world, and these small actions are also a living amends for those things I cannot rectify from my past.

I've heard it said before that you only have to change one thing when you come into the fellowship. That one thing is absolutely everything. The freedom this produces from fear, worry, anger, anxiety, depression, and stress, is nothing short of miraculous. Even if you believe there is no God and are a complete atheist, this course of living has immense agency over such feelings and stress. Our changes are gradual, and the work isn't insurmountable. It's a little bit at a time, with baby steps each and every day. In this way, changing everything becomes doable.

I wrote this book because, as a hurt person, I hurt others, and conversely, now, as a healed person, I live to help heal others. Over the years, I saw some inconsistencies in the modern fellowship and wanted to clarify some things to those undertaking this mission of hope. As I did, you'll find all kinds of sick people in the halls. They were often a detriment to recovery, yet through their example, they provided great lessons in what not to do.

At the onset of the fellowship there was a tight knit group of survivors who held together against all odds. When they saw someone trying, they'd help that person in many ways that we don't often do today in the fellowship. I've helped those earnest in their recovery with work and financial assistance. My judgment of another's character developed as my character changed. Sometimes I was disappointed when I missed some glaring flaws when I helped people because they used my kindness. This provided me

Paul Moore

with lessons in discernment, but I didn't allow it to jade me against all humanity.

I think as long as your conception of a higher power is loving, you will do alright. Eventually, as a father with a sober mind, I saw in myself what I wanted in a Higher Power. When I asked sober-minded Paul what he wanted for and from his children, the answer was simple. "I want the best for them." As we are created from a source of perfect love, it's inconceivable we would want less than the level best for us.

Sides of the triangle: Recovery, Unity, and Service

The AA symbol on the chips they hand out is a triangle, the base of which is recovery, and that is recovery from a seemingly hopeless state of mind through the 12 Steps.The sides represent unity and service. Unity is fellowship, and service is helping others in many ways. You'll find many like-minded folks in the fellowship, and if you search, you'll find your tribe of support—those people are available day and night to help guide you through this process. Funny enough, when one reaches out to another, all three sides of the triangle are working in synergy. Because of the paradox that is love, when one helps another, they are helping themselves, and when God joins, there's a force of nature greater than the sum of the parts.

Living in joy and serenity.

I'm going to say the best evidence I have is not my written words. It's the overall change in my energy. The smile on my face is evidence of the joy and serenity I experience. The laughter that fills the room I'm in is evidence. The forbearance to insults, slander, and opposing opinions that are met with love is the evidence. The peace of mind that allows solitude without loneliness is evidence. The fact I can have joy today, even in sadness, is evidence. Gratitude is evidence. My friends are evidence. My happy family is evidence. Being gainfully employed is evidence. Writing a book is evidence. Producing my podcast is evidence. When love is in abundance, it's quite evident.

"A cliche is a cliche because it works"

— Feige Gornish

RESOURCES

Fellowship Cliches

The cliches you'll see and hear around meetings, seem well, cliche. As an over-thinker, I've analyzed many of these very deeply, and they became cliche because they are truisms. They do apply and are usually the first things that come to mind when listening to another's problems with life. There are many, many more. I've purposely left some off the list for you to discover and overthink for yourself on your journey.

One day at a time: While this has great meaning even on the surface, this phrase reminds me to focus on the present, practice mindfulness, complete self-care, call my sponsor, and put one foot in front of the other and do what's necessary every day.

Easy does it: Very simple but with very deep meaning, all the things you'll need to do to recover if you sit back and look at them all at once are a lot! You are going to do a little at a time. Remember, Rome wasn't built in a day.

First things first: We often get hung up in the past or looking ahead to the future. This one is a reminder to come back to the present moment. Ask yourself, "What do I need to do now?" Maybe the answer is to attend a meeting. Maybe it's calling someone new and finding out how they are doing, and maybe it's time to eat ice cream and binge-watch mindless television. I can only do what I can do.

Live and let live: If I'm getting flustered from someone else or some situation, maybe I should ask if this is even my business and why I'm getting so riled up. People are going to have different opinions on everything: on how I should do my recovery, who they like for politicians, whether my book sucks, and how I betrayed my anonymity. These opinions are myriad, and once we've really done the steps, we will be in a position of neutrality with the world and the various opinions we disagree with. Today, I have a great amount of equanimity and don't get bothered much by others' opinions or even feel the need to educate others on how they are wrong. This saves me a lot of headaches!

But for the grace of God: This phrase reminds me to suspend my judgments. Maybe someone went further down the scale of addiction. Conversely, maybe they had one too many at the country club, they are there, and for whatever reason, they stopped. That's good enough. There's no negative net gain on society from them staying sober and trying to get better. When someone's story hasn't happened to me Y.E.T. (you're eligible too) I can simply say, but for the grace of God, go I and thank my lucky stars a similar situation didn't happen to me yet.

Let go and let God: This is apropos to the third step turning our will over to a greater power and practicing acceptance. When in doubt, pray and meditate for a solution.

In my opinion, meditation is the key to conscious contact with God.

Keep it Simple (Stupid, I prefer Spectacular, Special, Sensual, Spiritual, any S word that doesn't keep you calling yourself something negative) K.I.S.S. Keeping it simple might not mean easy. It's sometimes, in the beginning, a day-to-day trudge to get to a meeting and work the steps, but remember there is a great payoff for doing it—coupled with a terrible consequence to slacking off.

This too shall pass: Everything is transitory. Today's problems will eventually evaporate, and you now have tools to work on them, i.e., call your sponsor, go to a meeting, have a bite to eat, do a tenth step, pray, meditate, and/or help someone else.

Stick with the winners: If you are like me, you're going to have to dig deep and be observant of others' actions, not to judge, but to see who is actually happy. In the beginning, I'd have hung with the people with the coolest toys and hottest mates. I had to realize those things didn't make me happy. I eventually looked toward those who could solve problems with words, seemed peaceful, laughed and had fun, had good familial relations, and were not a burden on society. When I found those who were doing this, I realized they all had one thing in common. They prayed, meditated, and worked on the steps.

Keep right sized: Chances are if you are making a lot of statements with "I," "me," or "mine" in them, you're probably not in a good frame of mind. Sobriety is about keeping the ego in check, and being honest. When I'm making too many of these statements, it's good for me to stop and ask, "How are you?"

Faith without works is dead: This means praying is great, but it takes action to feel better. Just talking about how much you love God without spending some consideration on your fellow humans will not avail great results. I knew many very faithful and pious people who were still acting out in self-destructive manners. This is a program of action and change.

I came; I came to; I came to believe (steps 1, 2, 3): This phrase corresponds with steps one (honesty), two (open-mindedness), and three (willingness). For me, I knew I had a problem, I saw this work for others, and I asked for help.

To thine own self be true: This line comes from the play Hamlet by Shakespeare. I've found as you clear away the fears, you start to intuitively sense those things that make you uncomfortable. The discomfort applies very much to my character defects. For example, it might feel good at the time to gossip or brag in a conversation, but later, when I see the person I've gossiped about, I have trouble meeting their gaze. When I think about the situation, I realize maybe it'd be better if I didn't gossip about others, whether they deserve it or not.

Keep coming back…it works if you work it: This to me means sometimes I'm a bit thick or distracted. I'll have a better chance of doing the necessary work if I keep attending the fellowship, looking at my behavior, and making necessary changes.

Poor me... poor me, pour me another drink: I love to wallow in self-pity and the unfairness of life, or at least I did until I started realizing how uncomfortable a place this was to be. I've found the best and quickest cure for self-pity is simply asking any other human being this question: "How are you?" Next, I shut my mouth and listen to what they have to say.

We are only as sick as our secrets: The more I hide and distrust others, the more apart and alone I feel. While I might not want to give every human I meet the highlight reel of my most embarrassing moments, I can find those I trust to share these things with. My biggest foibles usually come out in the fifth step with a trusted sponsor, but I've found now that I don't behave in the manner I once did while sharing my transgressions is no longer that difficult, even with strangers.

Expect miracles: I got in the habit of having some hope. When I realized others have done this, I asked myself, "Why not me?" I stopped coming up with a terrible answer to this question because I've failed before: "Maybe I'm just no good." I started giving myself the same benefit of the doubt I'd give someone I was friendly with. When I started believing it was possible and having little successes, more successes built upon them. Even when I'd have bad days and get through them without a substance, I'd accept it as a small win.

90 meetings in 90 days...90/90: Attending 90 meetings in 90 days is simply good advice for getting in the habit of regular attendance. Doing this will show you different meetings and people and start a habit. The latest neuroscience shows that it takes 63 days to start a new habit. This also applies to the old adage, "birds of a feather flock together." If I hang with six millionaires, I'll probably be number seven. If I hang out with six drug addicts, I'll probably be the same.

Keep the plug in the jug: This one is pretty self-explanatory. Don't pick up a drink—or a drug!

Paul Moore

Be part of the solution, not the problem: This applies to actually using the program and the fellowship. Many newcomers and some people who have been around a while will use the meeting like group therapy and social hour and never partake in the solution that is the twelve steps. Bill Wilson describes this in the book, Twelve Steps and the Twelve Traditions as being a two-stepper, employing only steps one and twelve, and to try all the steps. Most of those who don't use all the steps to make a change in themselves will have tenuous sobriety, and usually not emotional sobriety.

Emotional sobriety: can also be described as equanimity, which is an even state of mind despite the adversity of daily existence. Problems of money, employment, relationships, and traffic, don't stop because we get sober and begin recovery. What changes is how we deal with issues as they arise. Seeking solutions such as lowering expectations on loved ones, having a good playlist ready for traffic, or an audiobook come into play. I recently spent fifteen hours in the emergency room for a relatively minor problem. I wasn't very flustered as I brought books to read and wrote while I was there. Similarly, the DMV wasn't terrible the last time I visited because I grabbed a coffee and had a friend to chat with while I waited. As we get through life's little conundrums, we develop better strategies for living with these things. We develop emotional sobriety, also known as recovery.

Live in the NOW: This is a practice of being present-minded and not living in the future of the past. Some of us are sicker than others: you'll encounter a lot of assholes in the program and people who make up their own ways to do things. I usually ask if they can show me their reasoning in the Alcoholics Anonymous literature. This usually stops them from pushing their own often skewed ideas onto me.

Just for today: Again, let's stay focused on right now or the solution, rather than the problem.

Pass it on: Help others and work Step 12 into your daily existence. Holding a door open, paying for the person's coffee next to you in line, picking a piece of trash off of the ground, giving someone new your number, taking their number, and texting hello. These are all examples of passing it on or paying it forward.

Another friend of Bill W.'s: Sometimes at meetings, or even out in public, people will ask if you are a friend of Bill W. Bill Wilson is the co-founder of Alcoholics Anonymous.

It takes time: T.I.M.E., Things I Must Earn: Though it seems like the first few months of sobriety take forever, time is relative. For those who we hurt with our addiction, a few months of sobriety isn't enough usually for them to understand how hard or how much work we need to put in to stay dry. We'd usually like to be forgiven quicker than it actually happens.

You will be amazed: This idea speaks of the promises listed after the ninth step in the book Alcoholics Anonymous aka the big book, the whole passage reads.

THE A.A. PROMISES

If we are painstaking about this phase of our development, we will be amazed before we are halfway through. We are going to know a new freedom and a new happiness. We will not regret the past nor wish to shut the door on it. We will comprehend the word serenity, and we will know peace. No matter how far down the scale we have gone, we will see how our experience can benefit others. That feeling of uselessness and self-pity will disappear. We will lose interest in selfish things and gain interest in our fellows. Self-seeking will slip away. Our whole attitude and outlook upon life will change. Fear of people and of economic insecurity will leave us. We will intuitively know how to handle situations which used to baffle us. We will suddenly realize that God is doing for us what we could not do for ourselves.

Are these extravagant promises? We think not. They are being fulfilled among us— sometimes quickly, sometimes slowly. They will always materialize if we work for them.

Respect the anonymity of others: Some people don't want everyone to know about their business, and AA has a tradition of staying anonymous in press, radio, and film. Overall, it is our own decision of how anonymous we wish to be, but saying you know Ted from work from Alcoholics Anonymous or another twelve-step fellowship may not go over very well.

If nothing changes, nothing changes: This maxim to me is not about being something or someone else. It's more about honestly assessing who I am and the changes that would improve my life. We all have areas where we could make some improvements: perhaps I wake up cranky, and kindly inform those I care about to let me have my coffee and wake up before engaging me in problems of the day. I might be acting less than honest in my interactions with others, hoping they will like me better. Changing oneself isn't becoming fake. It's aligning more with our internal values.

You will intuitively know: this one once again is a variation on the ninth steps promises. We will intuitively know how to solve problems that baffle us. This knowing comes from hard-won experience. We typically gain this experience in turmoil and failure.

The last time they disparaged me at work, I told them all to go to hell, and I was fired. What can I do differently next time that would be more helpful? Perhaps I'll keep my mouth closed while I'm angry and keep my job while seeking other employment. This is another reason it's called practicing the steps. Sometimes these seemingly obvious solutions we are oblivious to until someone points them out. My friend John came into recovery in his twenties and wasn't fully prepared for adulting. He'd go to meetings and park illegally to avoid being late, and he'd therefore receive parking tickets. Someone finally pointed out during his complaining perhaps he could leave earlier and park legally. He marked this as quite an epiphany and said, "Gee, why didn't I think of that?"

Turn it over: This instruction corresponds to Step 3, but I'd also say Step 11. In Step 3, we make a decision to turn our life and will over to the care of God as we understand him. At this point, I had no real idea of what God's will was. It took research, meditation, house cleaning of my resentments, and more to start realizing what the mysterious deity's will was for me. Now, when I'm angry and cannot see a solution to my anger, I talk to trusted advisors, meditate and ask for a solution or acceptance or both. I make a decision on how to act or react to the problem and go with what gives me more peace.

Sobriety (recovery) is a journey…not a destination: I was always destination-oriented. I'd think, "When I get five years sober, I'll be happy.

When I get the promotion at work, I'll be happy. When I achieve my goal, I'll be happy. When I get a degree, I'll be happy." I got all those things at times in my journey, but I wasn't happy when I achieved them. It turns out happiness was an inside job, which took a change in my thinking process. Here's a simple observation of what it looks like to appreciate the journey over the destination. Why do I need to rush cooking to eat? Because I'm starving while preparing the meal. I started preparing the meal while I wasn't starving. I'd have a snack before the preparation. I'd peel each potato and carrot with care. I'd choose the spices I liked best. I began to enjoy both the process and the meal more because of the care and attention I exerted. Conversely, I ate less because I ate slower, savoring each bite. Part of getting the degree or the goal is the day-to-day process of working on these things. Being present for these activities can be quite enjoyable.

Don't quit 5 minutes before the miracle happens: This adage means to keep trying—even when things don't go your way. Employ the tools you've learned, or ask someone how they got through these troubled times. Those who do suffer relapses while still trying these steps need to lower their level of pride, suit up and try again, even if you think, "Oh God, I lost all my sober time." Did you really? The experiences you've had cannot be taken away from you. Any failure simply takes a little courage to get over. The ability to go further takes an honest reassessment of where your work was lacking.

Before you say, "I can't, say "I'll try:" This direction applies to having an open mind—even if you think it can't work. I thought prayer and meditation were stupid when I was told to try them, but I couldn't argue it wasn't working for those who told me to try. The people who meditated and prayed were doing things I couldn't: laughing, smiling, solving problems constructively, having good familial relations, and not being a burden on those around them. These things they could do without a substance, and I could not. I figured maybe it was worth trying what they did rather than looking down my nose at their solution because they obviously had one.

There are no coincidences in AA: Serendipities will start occurring. I've heard them also called "God shots." Freud, in Totems and Taboo, said the human mind is prone to an erroneous connection where no connections exist. This was also stated before good knowledge of quantum physics. I'll let you do your own investigation there. My point is it doesn't matter. If I feel synchronicity has occurred because the person in the meeting told the exact right story at precisely the right time, and it was exactly what I needed to hear, and was helpful, could that not be God helping me and loving me? It certainly doesn't hurt to think so. I think Freud was both right and wrong about the associations we make. However, if it is helpful to me in living a happy, productive life, why not use it?

If God seems far away, who moved?: Asking this question can be a daily check for me that reveals my spiritual condition. Aligning my will with the God of my understanding which involves a lot of things like practicing forgiveness, lowering expectations on outcomes, and being kind and charitable, usually helps place me outside of the ego zone. When I'm not making a lot of statements beginning with "I," "Me," or "Mine," I'm probably more connected to another more majestic source.

If it works, don't fix it: This statement is pretty self-explanatory but a good reminder while we are still thinking in doom and gloom. Maybe the outcome will be just fine. I'll keep practicing what I've learned and see what comes.

Nothing is so bad, a drink (or drug, or gambling, or meaningless sex) won't make it worse: I've added a few of my own in the parentheses. As bad as I feel during any moment of recovery, I know that after the mild amusement of one of my vices passes, I'll feel much, much worse.

Keep an open mind: Why go? First, it'll never work when I haven't really given it a chance. All things occur in recovery from time, effort, and practice. I, who have an instant gratification fetish from years of push-button relief from using drugs, might think that life should be fine after a week or two of practice. And yet, anything worthwhile takes time.

Willingness is the key: People don't usually think very hard when asked what they are willing to do to feel good. They quickly blurt out, "Anything!" These changes require a really deep look at willingness. Here are some deep questions about recovery, "Am I willing to pray? Am I willing to write out my inadequacies? Am I willing to practice this?"

Willingness is one big key to recovery. Cheer up. What you'll have to do isn't insurmountable, and you can do it a little at a time, so easy does it.

Let it begin with me: If I'm complaining about something I don't like, I can ask a simple question. "What can I do to make it better?" Asking this is simple but not easy because usually, the answer involves work. I have been lazy for most of my life, and I would rather someone else get things done for me. Over the years, I've asked my family, the government, therapists, and others to do the work on my behalf. The truth is recovery is like working out. It's something you'll need to do for yourself.

Practice an attitude of gratitude: This is good advice for lots of reasons. I once needed to have the new iPhone. I'd look at it all shiny, read the new features, and say, "I've got to have that!" Maybe I couldn't really afford it, and maybe my old one worked just fine still. The truth is, after three days of showing off the new iPhone, it didn't really bring me any great sense of comfort or satisfaction. I like having many guitars, but I usually ask myself, "How much I actually play the four I already own?" when salivating over a new one. Today I'm still using an iPhone that's two models behind the newest release. I'm grateful I have it, it's purple, and works just fine. Always looking at what I want rather than practicing being grateful for what I have never led to happiness.

You are not alone: This sense starts coming from attendance at meetings and being among others in the fellowship. When I listen to what other people have been through, I feel connected because they are like me. This is further fostered by sharing more personal facts with another human being in Step 5. While some of these personal facts are embarrassing, and I'd like to keep them hidden, when I trust myself enough to reveal them, I usually learn the people I share these facts with have experienced similar events.

"We understand ... that what constitutes the dignity of a craft is that it creates a fellowship, that it binds men together and fashions for them a common language."

— Antoine de Saint-Exupery

Fellowship Acronyms

AA = Absolute Abstinence…**AA** = Adventurers Anonymous…
AA = Altered Attitudes… **AA** = Altruistic Action…
AA = Attitude Adjustment…**AA's-R-US** = Alcoholics Anonymous Recovery Unity Service.
ABC = Acceptance, Belief, Change.
ACTION = Any Change To Improve Our Natures.
ACTION = Any Change Toward Improving One's Nature.
ADDICT = Anybody Doing Drugs In Compulsive Trouble.
AFGE = Another F****** Growth Experience.
ALCOHOLICS = A Life Centered On Helping Others Live In Complete Sobriety.
ANGER = A No Good Energy Rising.
ANONYMOUS = Actions Not Our Names Yield Maintenance Of Unity & Service.
ASK = Ass-Saving Kit.
BAR = Beware Alcohol, Run…**BAR** = Beware Alcohol Ruin.
BIG BOOK = Believing In God Beats Our Old Knowledge.
BS = Before Sobriety.
BUT = Being Unconvinced Totally.
CALM = Can Anger Leave Me.
CARE = Comforting And Reassuring Each Other.
CHANGE = Choosing Honesty Allows New Growth Everyday.
CIA = Catholic Irish Alcoholic.
CLEAN = Completely Leaving Every Addiction Now!
COURAGE = 'Cause of Using Recovery's A Great Effort.
CRAP = Carry Resentments Against People.
DEAD = Drinking Ends All Dreams.
DENIAL = Don't Even Notice I Am Lying.
DENIAL = Don't Even Notice It's A Lie.
DETACH = Don't Even Think About Changing Him/Her.

DT'S = Don't Think Shit.

DUES = Desperately Using Everything But Sobriety.

EDI not DIE = Easy Does It not Does It Easy.

EGO = Easing God Out...**EGO** = Edging God Out.

F.E.A.R. (Face Everything And Recover) There are lots of acronyms for fear; this one I like because it's positive and brings growth.

F.E.A.R. (False Evidence Appearing Real): Everything we experience is from our own perspective. We might take something someone says as a sideways personal attack, and it is not. When I was behaving poorly, a coworker could tell a story that would barely touch on my behavior, and I'd assume they somehow knew of my own embarrassment and were doing it on purpose. This was paranoia.

F.E.A.R. (Fuck Everything And Run) This one, of course, is the opposite of the last one.

F_CKED = Feeling Useless 'Cause I'm Kicking Every Drug.

FAILURE = Fearful, Arrogant, Insecure, Lonely, Uncertain, Resentful, Empty.

FAITH = Fear Ain't In This House...**FAITH** = Facing An Inner Truth Heals,

FAITH = Fear And Insecurity? Trust Him!

FAITH = For An Instant Trust Him...**FAITH** = Fantastic Adventure In Trusting Him.

FAMILY = Father And Mother I Love You.

FEAR = Failure Expected And Received.

FEAR = Feelings Every Alcoholic Rejects.

FEAR = Feelings Expressed Allows Relief.

FEAR = Fighting Ego Against Reality.

FEAR = Forget Everything And Run.

FEAR = Forgetting Everything's All Right.

FEAR = Frantic Effort to Appear Real.

FEAR = Frantic Efforts to Appear Recovered.

FINE = Faithful, Involved, Knowledgeable, and Experienced.

FINE = F–cked, Insecure, Neurotic, and Emotional. FOG = Fear of God.

FINE = Feeling Insecure, Neurotic, and Emotional.

FINE = Feeling Insecure, Numb, and Empty.

FINE = Frantic, Insane, Nuts, and Egotistical.

FINE = Freaked out, Insecure, Neurotic, and Emotional.

FINE = Frustrated, Insecure, Neurotic, and Emotional.

GIFT = God Is Forever There.

GIFTS = Getting It From The Steps.

GOD = Get Out Devil.

GOD = Go On Dreaming.

GOD = Good Orderly Direction.

GOD = Group Of Drug Addicts. GOYA = Get Off Your Ass.

GOD = Group Of Drunks.

GUT = God's Undeniable Truths.

HALT = Honestly, Actively, Lovingly Tolerant.

HALT = Hope, Acceptance, Love, and Tolerance.

HALT = Horny, Arrogant, Lazy, and Tragic: If you're any one of these, get to a meeting!

HALT = Hungry, Angry, Lonely, Tired: Fix these situations before you make any decisions.

HALTS = Hungry, Angry, Lonely, Tired, and Stupid.

HALTS FEAR = Hope, Acceptance, Love, and Tolerance Stops Forgetting That Everything's All Right.

HEART = Healing, Enjoying, and Recovering Together.

HELP = Her Ever Loving Presence.

HELP = His Ever Loving Presence.

HELP = Hope, Encouragement, Love, and Patience.

HOPE = Hang On! Peace Exists.

HOPE = Happy Our Program Exists.

HOPE = Hearing Other Peoples' Experience.

HOW = Honest, Open-Minded, and Willing.

HOW = Honesty, Open-Mindedness, Willingness; that's how we do it.

ISM = I Sabotage Myself.

ISM = I Sponsor Myself.

ISM = I, Self, Me.

ISM = Incredibly Short Memory.

ISM = InSide Me.

KISS = Keep It Simple, Stupid.

KISS = Keep It Simple, Sugar.

KISS = Keep It Simple, Sweetheart.

KISS = Keeping It Simple, Spiritually.

LET GO = Leave Everything To God, Okay?

LOVE = Living Our Victories Everyday...

MMM = Meetings, Meditation, and Masturbation: recommended for the first year.

NEW = Nothing Else Worked.   **NOW** = No Other Way.

NOWHERE or NOW HERE

NUTS = Not Using The Steps.

OUR = Openly Using Recovery.

PACE = Positive Attitudes Change Everything.

PAID = Pitiful And Incomprehensible Demoralization.

PAIN = Pause And Invite New.

PHD = Pretty Heavy Drinker.

PMS = Poor Me Syndrome.

PMS = Pour More Scotch.

PRIDE = Personal Recovery Involves Defeating Ego.

PROGRAM = People Relying On God Relaying A Message.

RAGE = Real Angry Gut-level Ego.

RELAPSE = Recovery Exits Life And Program Seem Empty.

RELATIONSHIP = Really Exciting Love Affair Turns Into Outrageous Nightmare, Sobriety Hangs In Peril.

RID = Restless, Irritable, and Discontented.

RUN + I = RUIN.....**RUIN – I** = RUN (Let God run the show 'cause I ruin everything.)

SASTO = Some Are Sicker Than Others.

SHIT = Simply How I'm Thinking.

SLIP = Sobriety Loses Its Priority.

SOB = Sober Old Bag.

SOB = Sober Old Bastard.

SOB = Sober Old Biker.

SOB = Sober Old Bitch.

SOBER = Son Of A Bitch, Everything's Real.

SOBER = Staying Off Booze Enjoying Recovery.

SOBRIETY = Stay Off Booze, Recovery Is Everything To You.

SOLUTIONS = Saving Our Lives Using The Inventory Of Needed Steps.

SPONSOR = Sober Person Offering Newcomers Suggestions On Recovery.

STAR = Start Talking About Recovery.

STEPS = Solutions To Every Problem in Sobriety.

STEPS = Solutions To Every Problem, Sober.

STOP = Sicker Than Other People.

TIME = Things I Must Earn. This is one of the most hated acronyms to hear while you are feeling miserable. Things like trust returning take not only effort and practice but also time.

TIME = This I Must Earn.

TRUST = Try Relying Upon The Steps.

WASP = Worry Anger Self Pity.

WILLING = When I (Let Go & Let God) (Live & Let Live) I Normally Grow.

WILLING = When I Live Life, I Need God.

WISDOM = When Into Self, Discover Our Motives.

WORK = What Our Recovery Knows.

WORRY = Wrong Or Right Remain Yourself. YET = You're Eligible Too.

YET = You'll End Up There.

"One day you will tell your story of how you overcame what you went though and it will be someone else's survival guide."

— Brené Brown

Referenced Books and Recommended Resources

The Twelve Steps and The Twelve Traditions by Bill Wilson

Recovery Russell Brand

Your Erroneous Zones by Wayne Dyer

The Wim Hof Method: Activate Your Full Human Potential, Wim Hof

Joe and Charlie App

About the Author

Paul Moore
www.beyondfellowship.com

Paul Moore has been practicing and mostly failing at recovery for thirty years of his life. In many attempts and trials and errors, he found a comprehensive way of working these steps of Alcoholics Anonymous.

In four short years, Paul went from hopelessly suicidal, to happy and comfortable in his own skin. He went from unemployable to seeking his second certification as a substance use disorder counselor. Once too lazy to commit to regular hygiene, he graduated to writing this book, certifying a sober living center, creating a recovery channel on YouTube, researching book two, and working full time treating addicts and alcoholics toward recovery.

He lives in Coventry Rhode Island with his wife Graca, two adult children pursuing education, and the family's four cats. His eldest daughter is married and raising his two grandchildren. This family once torn to pieces from the use and abuse of drugs and alcohol is now united again. Things are not perfect, but they are getting pretty close.

In addition to writing this book: Paul is finishing up his hours for licensing as a chemical dependency specialist, working on an upcoming book on recovery, and plans are underway to open a small recovery center based on his many years of experience. The main reason for this book is his knowledge a happy existence can be built from the wreckage and chaos of lifelong addiction, and mental illness. When you climb up to a higher rung on the ladder, it's necessary to show others this place exists.

This book has been written, edited, and published at his own expense as an amends to the world for living a very sordid existence. The electronic version is offered free of charge to any who will use it.

Connect with Paul at pmoore@beyondfellowship.com.

Courses & Community Support

Awaken Your Inner Author, www.awakenyourinnerauthor.com

Download Melissa's Magic system to finally write the book that's trapped in your mind and heart.

As aspiring authors, we dream of our book creating a movement for the world and financial freedom for ourselves. But far too often, what happens instead is the soul-crushing experience of publishing your book only to have sales fall flat, momentum stunted, and your potentially life-changing book reaches precious few people. We are dedicated to making sure your story ends quite differently -- with you creating the impact and income that you desire from your book. That's where the publishing partnership with Ultimate Vida comes in. Grounded with decades of experience in online marketing and building sound business models around books, we help authors sidestep land mines and reach their goals by providing actionable data (like title and cover testing), a deep and intimate understanding of who your audience actually is (which is bound to surprise you), strategic advice on offerings beyond the book, and ongoing monthly income opportunities that far exceed book royalties. Reach out to melissa@uncorpedinfluence.com to discuss strategies to make a splash with your book and incorporate the Ultimate Vida community experience and course as a new revenue stream.

Join the Ultimate Vida Freedom Circle

Your Secret Weapon To Kiss Your Job Goodbye in as Little as 77 Days, Build an Online Tribe, and Leave a Legacy

As an Ultimate Vida Freedom Circle Member, you can:

- Create a baseline of time and financial freedom while doing work you love
- Access proprietary data and strategies to blissfully use your newfound recovery as a guide in your entrepreneurial journey
- Get FREE access to our flagship Freedom Blueprint course, which sells on its own for $1,500
- Use your newfound freedom to focus on health, wellness, relationships, and purpose...the things that make life worth living
- Connect with the world's most epic tribe of freedom seekers to enrich your life, help you achieve your goals, and form lifelong friendships
- Earn supplemental income or even life-changing monthly money by referring others into the community

ULTIMATE
Vida

Enjoy the Community for FREE for 14 days!
www.ultimatevida.com/fellowship